Dear Santa

gawa-ku Tokyo 141-0021
n

JULENISSEN
1440 DROBAK
Norway

BY AIR MAIL 航空
PAR AVION

Father Christmas
N - JULENISSEN
1440 D -
NORVÈGE

France : LETTRE
International PRIORITAIRE

LUFTPOST

Julenis
Torget
1440
- Norwe

Dear Santa

BIRGER SIVERTSEN

JB

JOHN BLAKE

Published by John Blake Publishing Ltd,
3 Bramber Court, 2 Bramber Road,
London W14 9PB, England

www.johnblakepublishing.co.uk

First published in hardback in 2010

ISBN: 978 1 84358 250 2

British Library Cataloguing-in-Publication Data:

A catalogue record for this book is available from the British Library.

Design by www.envydesign.co.uk

Printed in Spain by Graficas 94 SL

1 3 5 7 9 10 8 6 4 2

All images courtesy of Birger Sivertsen, except pages 2, 11, 36, 131, 157,
and 169 which are courtesy of Getty Images

Papers used by John Blake Publishing are natural, recyclable products made from
wood grown in sustainable forests. The manufacturing processes conform
to the environmental regulations of the country of origin.

Every attempt has been made to contact the relevant copyright-holders,
but some were unobtainable. We would be grateful if the appropriate
people could contact us.

Contents

Dear Santa...
Introduction

Every year, the Norwegian Postal Services receive over 30,000 letters and postcards from all over the world, addressed to Santa Claus. Sent by both children and adults, the letters are funny, sad, sweet, rude, joyful, greedy and hopeful. From lists of Christmas wishes to questions for Santa Claus, in this book you can read some of these wonderful letters, and maybe send one yourself when you are done...

Dear Julenissen,

We are a group of American Girl Scouts who are learning about Christmas in Norway. We have been reading about you and about your country and hope to learn even more about what it is like to be a young girl in Norway. Merry Christmas from the U.S.

Fondly,
Daisy Scout Troop 3130
Whitney EMMA EmiLee
Amanda Taylor Diana Madison
Breohne, Love

Caro Babbo Natale,
I wish not to have holes in my teeth for the rest of my
life so I can eat as much candy I want all Christmas.
Christmas hugs from Violetta, ITALY.

Dear Father Christmas,
This year I have only one wish, and that is
to learn how to fly with my body!
Your Ewelina, POLAND.

Cher Père Nöel,
I wish for a helicopter ride over Paris. Then I want
it to land on the top of the Eiffel Tower. I don't
think anyone has ever done that before me?
Greetings from Martial, FRANCE.

Dear Santa,
If it's possible I wish to master the art of walking on
water. Then I can walk while daddy sails the old wooden
boat. And then I don't have to scoop out the water.
From Joshua, USA.

DEAR SANTA

Hallo Santa,
I want to become a really good police officer.
Greetings from Sasha, UKRAINE.

Dear Santa Claus,
I would like Norwegian kroner for Christmas.
Greetings from Morita, JAPAN.

Dear Santa Claus,
I wish for a TV in my room, my brother Herman wishes
for it the most, and I've just gotten a new brother called
August, and I think he wants clothes.
Greeting from Johan, NORWAY.

Caro Babbo Natale,
I wish for a baby next Summer!
Greetings from Sofia, ITALY.

Dear Santa,

I wish for a Playstation 2 for Christmas. Mum says it's too expensive for her, but what if you and dad chip in? Greetings from Ashby, AUSTRALIA.

Dear Santa Claus,

You only come to Poland on December 6th, but in other countries you come Christmas Eve. I want you to come to me on Christmas Eve as well! Greetings from Natalka, POLAND.

Dear Santa,

Hi, my name is John and I'm 13 years old. I want you to make peace in the world. Kisses from John, GREECE.

In Italy, Santa is called Babbo Natale, meaning Father Christmas. Children put a pair of their shoes by the door on the day before Christmas, and the following morning they find them filled with small gifts and sweets.

Dear Santa,

Merry Christmas and
A happy New Year 2009!

MERRY
CHRIST
MAS

HAPPY
NEW
YEAR
2009

Po

Sincerely yours

To Santa,

We would like to receive more presents, because we don't get very many for Christmas. We're called Hanne and Camilla. Hanne is 10 years old and Camilla is 9 years old. Hanne has a boyfriend called Thomas Andre, and Camilla's boyfriend is called Tom. We want you to buy stuff for them too, is that OK? We're doing great! Greetings from Hanne and Camilla, NORWAY.

Dear Santa Claus,

Please don't give me a cat or a book for Christmas, because I already have that! I would rather have skis, a bike, a dog or a CD-player.
From Pawel, POLAND.

Dear Santa,

It's me! I wish for more teddy bears. Do you know what, mum says that I have 100 teddies, but I only have 40.
Hugs from Julia, SWEDEN.

DEAR SANTA

To Santa,
I would like to meet Roy-Erling, have siblings
and my guitar tuned.
Best wishes Anne-Karin, NORWAY.

Dear Santa Claus,
Would you please give my dear brother a football?
Love Werner, GERMANY.

To Santa,
What I want most of all is to have my cosy
teddy bear back. I lost him.
Regards from Karoline, NORWAY.

Dear Santa Claus,
I wish for longer hair. Like Amy's, but
perhaps a little longer.
Best regards, Catherine, ENGLAND.

Dear Santa Claus,
Most of all I would like to see you and your reindeer
coming down from the sky and flying over the roofs.
Yours Aki, JAPAN.

Dear Santa Claus,
I only wish for one thing, and that is for IKEA to open
here, and give me a job when I'm grown up.
From Klaudia, ESTONIA.

Dear Santa Claus,
I want a dollhouse for Christmas. And a doll
that can pee, grunt, yell and walk.
Greetings from Marthe, NORWAY.

Dear Father Christmas,
I hope you and the reindeer are fine. This year I'm going to ask you for a special present. I've just turned 15, and I know that there are kids who are younger than me who need presents more than me. Therefore, I must almost insist that you give the presents that are meant for me to all these kids, and if possible in my name. I thank you, and wish you a very merry Christmas!
Love from Maude, USA.

Liebe Weihnachtsmann,
I want sausages for dinner every day all year round.
From Elsa, GERMANY.

Dear Santa,
I wish you a merry Christmas, and then I wish for a quieter older sister! Say hello to Rudolph.
Greetings from Fride, NORWAY.

Dear father Christmas,
Most of all I would like a fishing rod that constantly catches fish.
Your Reinhard, GERMANY.

Dear Santa Claus,
My biggest wish is that you and I will
sing karaoke together. Is that OK?
Love Hitomi, JAPAN.

Dear Santa,
My name is Ida Emilie and I'll turn nine in January.
I'm really looking forward to Christmas, and thus I send
you my list of Christmas wishes. I want dancing
skates, a slide, a yellow fish, peace on earth and
a boyfriend. Preferably Haakon.
Greetings from Ida Emilie, NORWAY.

Dear Santa,

I sincerely want a family who can clean up after themselves. I already have a family, and I would like to keep it, as long as it's tidy! It's always so messy here and full of crumbs everywhere! I want the same family, but they must be tidy, and I want to learn how to be tidy as well! That's my wish this year; could you please make it come true?

Greetings from Ingvild, NORWAY.

Hey sweet Santa,

My list of Christmas wishes:

1) Peace on earth, and possibly in other places of the universe.

2) No hunger on earth, and possibly in other places of the universe.

3) That all the bad people go to Jokkmokk in Sweden.

4) That everybody will be nice to one another.

5) Win 1 million kroner.

Best regards Espen, NORWAY.

Dear Santa,

I wish for a dog that has a much bigger head than body.

Love Irina, POLAND.

Dear Santa Claus,

I've been very good this year and thus have made a long list of Christmas wishes. If I get four of these things, I'll continue believing in you for another year.

Yours Valentina, ITALY.

Per babbo Natale,

If possible I wish to get the best grades in my class as long as I'm in school.

Yours Antonio, ITALY.

Dear Santa Claus,

My biggest wish is to have a trampoline, and that you'll find a place to put it. We don't have much space.

From Nicholas, HONG KONG.

Mr. Santa,

My biggest wish is that you'll come to a party at my place on December 26th.

Love Arisa, JAPAN.

DEAR SANTA

....

Dear Santa Claus,
I want a nice sister and generous parents!
Love Jasmine, BELGIUM.
P.S. I'll be 12 on Christmas Eve.

Dear Santa Claus,
Thank you very much for the presents last year.
This year I would like to have twice as many.
Love Niohmi, ENGLAND.

BIRGER SIVERTSEN

Caro Babbo Natale,

If it's OK that you don't give me presents for many
years, I'll save them up so you can give me the greatest
present of all when I'm grown up: The Oscar award!

Best regards Chiara, ITALY.

PS: You do know what the Oscar award is, right?

Dear Santa Claus,

I wish for 15 things, but most of all hair stripes (stripes
in my hair) in a light orange colour.

Big kiss and hug from Diana, NORWAY.

Dear Santa,

I want a goldfish, but I don't think you'll be able to
bring it all the way from the North Pole to California.
However, you seem to be able to do everything!

From Mary Ann, USA.

Dear Father Christmas,

Could you make me a lot prettier than Sabrina?
That's my biggest and only wish!

Love Diana, GIBRALTAR.

Dear Santa Claus,
Mum says that I'm too young to have a cell phone,
but I'm actually nine. If I get it from you, she can't
say anything. Therefore it's my greatest wish.
Love Carina, SWEDEN.
PS: Preferably a Nokia.

Dear Santa,
My sister lives in Essex in England with her husband
and children, and I live in Amsterdam with my parents.
Since it's so expensive to make phone calls, I want you to
build us a super walkie-talkie so we can talk together
every night. Thanking you in anticipation.
Josie, HOLLAND.

Dear Santa Claus,
I want ducks without teeth. No more than four,
but that'll do perfectly.
Love Elin, SWEDEN.
PS: I'll take geese if it's a hard task,
but remember, no teeth!

Dear Santa...

Lists of Christmas wishes
from troubled areas

Dear Santa Claus,

Merry Christmas. What are you doing right now?
I hope that the charming and beautiful landscape of
Norway gives you energy for everything you have to do
soon. You probably expect that all the letters you receive
are from children, but I'm 24 years old. The last four
years I sent you a letter every Christmas and made you
drawings. I'm very interested in Norway and hope that
one day (maybe in the near future) I'll be able to visit
this wonderful country and live there forever. Perhaps you
can help me with this and make my dreams come true. I
hope that my dream will become a reality if I pray to God
repeatedly. With the authority that you have, I'm sure
that you can give much help and assistance also in this
connection. I'll be grateful if you can send me books
about Henrik Ibsen and his works. You may be surprised
to receive such a wish, but it's because I'm a despaired
and tormented person who has missed faith and
happiness every Christmas throughout my childhood and
adolescence. I have a lot of information about Norway,
from Kristiansand to Hammerfest, His Majesty Harald
V to Solskjaer, from A to AA, and much more, like for
example Svalbard. I know that it may be difficult to
make my wish come true, but it's for these troubles and
solutions you earn people's love and respect. Santa, let
the love and strength of your forefathers (the Vikings) be
your only guide to helping a person who's lost the sparkle
of life, and who waits for you, the reindeer, and your
shining, noble sledge. Please, help me and let my eyes

sparkle by the sight of Droebak and Oslo. I beg you to send me a personal response. I'm looking forward to hearing from you as soon as possible, have a very merry Christmas, and I thank you from the bottom of my emotions.

Yours Muhammed, IRAQ.

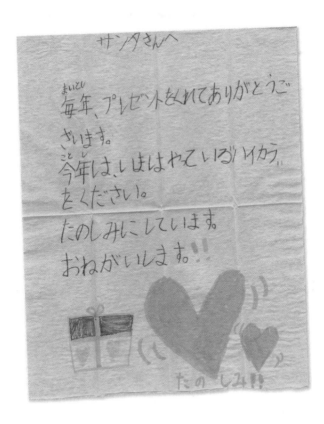

Dear Santa,

We live in a poor hamlet, and mamma and papa
don't have money for Christmas presents this year either.
Therefore I wish that my siblings and I will have just
a tiny mini present from you. Just a small one.
Best regards Danid, RUSSIA.

Dear Father Christmas,

Thanks a lot for sending me a postcard. After reading the
card I felt that I needed to discuss my problem with you.
As you know my country has been boycotted by the
international society so we need necessary foods such
as milk, cheese, vitamins and even more important
nutrition products. My family has a great need for these
basic products. May I by the way mention that I'm a
Christian and have three children? I'll be very grateful
if you can help me and my family with the most
necessary things such as milk, cheese and vitamins
and whatever you believe is necessary for my
family. Receive my best regards and wishes.
Sincerely Munther, IRAQ.

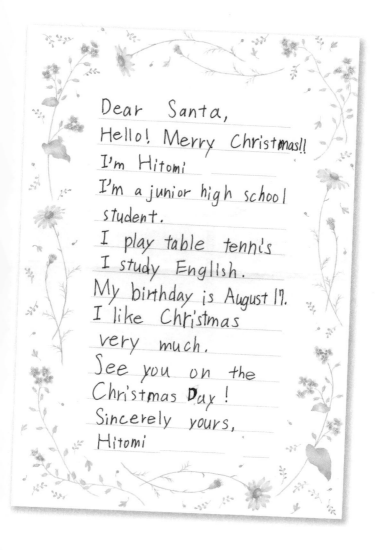

Dear Santa,
Hello! Merry Christmas!!
I'm Hitomi
I'm a junior high school
student.
I play table tennis
I study English.
My birthday is August 17.
I like Christmas
very much.
See you on the
Christmas Day!
Sincerely yours,
Hitomi

Mr. Santa Claus,

Me and my entire family will be deeply [and] eternally grateful if you can send us a visa for a good country to live in plus plane tickets and some money for food. Preferably in Scandinavia. I hope you'll be able to personally assist us for a couple of weeks so we can find a house and some jobs.

Best regards P.T., ETHIOPIA.

Dear Santa...

Good advice for Santa Claus

Dear Santa,

I would like a lot of stuff. I'm now preparing for Christmas. Are you coming Christmas Eve? I want a handball, May-Britt Andersen's latest CD, a new writing desk, my own slide, socks, handball clothes and a wallet. We're away Christmas Eve. You can come, but we've gone on vacation. We're at grandmother and grandfather's. Use the door, not the chimney because they light a fire in it. Welcome!

Love Kristina, NORWAY.

Dear Santa,

This year I'll be at my grandparents place again. Josefine is there too. See you!

Greetings from Max, NORWAY.

Babbo Natale,

I think the reason I didn't get that many presents last year was bad landing conditions on the roof. My advice to you this Christmas is that you land on the playground to the left, because then you and the reindeer can just walk from there. Is that OK?

Lots of greetings Patrik, ITALY.

Dear Santa,

I hope you're doing great. I wish for a bird that can sing. Our chimney is quite small so you better use the doorbell. Have a nice Christmas.
Lots of Christmas hugs from Beth, NORWAY.

Santa Claus!

Be careful when you come. Our dog bit the postman. And he wears a uniform. Dogs don't like those. He'll bite your bum. Could you take off the uniform?
Sincerely Jim, USA.

Dear Santa,

This year I would like a horse! Tie it to the fence behind the house. It cannot go down the chimney. It's impossible!
Lots of greetings from Jordan, ENGLAND.

Papa Noel!

I want the exact same clothes as Carmen just got, and then I want a bra that's a little stuffed. Ask your wife if you have any problems.
Regards from Marina, SPAIN.

29

CARO BABBO NATALE
VORREY IL BORSELINO DELL'INTER
IO VORREY 20€ EURO.

E ANCHE IL LIBRO DELL'INTER.
E LE MACCHINE DI LEGO,
E I GORMITI. LORENZO
TASCA.

Papa Noel,

This year I wish for an important thing: Could you press my teeth together so I don't have to wear a brace anymore? And remember that we've moved; the people who bought our house don't have kids. So you don't have to go there.

Gratefully Alexandre, SPAIN.

Dear Santa Claus,

There's no light in the room where we have the chimney. So you have to walk carefully! And then I'm going to put a bottle of daddy's whisky in the hall. You can just take that with you, after you've delivered the presents.

Love Brian, ENGLAND.

Dear Santa Claus,

In all pictures you have a huge behind. If your behind is really that big you won't be able to go down the chimney. But if you take off your clothes and rub your behind with oil, you'll probably be able to slide down.

But I don't know how you'll get up again.

Regards Andrew, NEW ZEALAND.

Dear Santa Claus,

I write to you because I've become allergic to animals
this year. Therefore you can't park your reindeer on the
roof like you usually do. Neither can you come inside
the house after touching the reindeer. Please park the
reindeer on our neighbor's roof and throw the
presents here. If you whistle I'll come.

Love Ewa, POLAND.

Dear Santa Claus,

I hope that you and the reindeer will have
a nice Christmas. Could you only give my brother
books for Christmas? They have to be bad if
they're not really spooky!

Love Guillaume, FRANCE.

P.S: We read in English too.

Caro Babbo Natale.

I wish for my daddy to stop dying his hair, it looks
really phony. If you do the same, I'll say: Get out!

Sincerely Claudia, ITALY.

Twinkle green ＊＊

Of each shines small, and it
will become big light before long.

TO

JLE. NISSEN
40 DROBAK

orway

BY AIR MAIL 航空
PAR AVION

NIPPON 110

TAKANAWA TOKYO
20.XI.08.'12

日本郵便

Dear Santa Claus,

You know that I want a dog, and you know that mum and dad don't want one. But when they see him they'll probably want me to keep him. Therefore it's not wise to go down the chimney with him because then he'll get dirty, and mum and dad will get upset. Can't you just go down the chimney yourself and say that my present is tied to the mailbox pole? Then it'll be alright.

Regards your friend Scott, ENGLAND.

Dear Santa Claus,

You're nice and I'm looking forward to seeing you. My Christmas wish is that all children who live in Africa may receive a present. Take care during Christmas.

Love Asle, NORWAY.

Caro Babbo Natale,

Why can't your wife deliver presents one year so you can experience what it's like to celebrate Christmas? I suggest that you ask her!

Love Cirinna, ITALY.

Dear Santa.

We send you a special gift. You can use it if it becomes so cold that your fingers get stiff and your nose red. Pick up the rubber bands and twist them hard around your fingers several times. When you remove them your fingers are warm.

Best regards Florian, DENMARK.

In Japan, Santa is called Santa Claus or just Santa. Children often call him "Santa no ojisan" which means "Uncle Santa".

SANTA CLAUS
SANTA'S WORKSHOP
THE NORTH POLE

KRIS Kringle
Santas Works
NORTH POLE

UNITED STATES
POSTAL SERVICE®
PAR AVION
AIRMAIL

KRIS KRINGLE
NORTH POLE LN
THE NORTH POLE

DANIEL

SANT
100 SAN
THE

Dear Santa...
I've been good!

Dear Santa,

Is it you who decides who's been good this year or is it mum and dad? Or do you have some sort of council on the North Pole who decide everything? I'm sure it can't be either or because there must be an in between, or is it that we who've been in between don't get any presents?

Sincerely Klaudynka, HUNGARY.

To Santa,

I've been kind all year so now I deserve everything I want. I want: A snowboard, PC, new bike, new skates, machinegun, flamethrower, Terminator 2 movie, Ace Ventura 2 movie, 1000 kroner and Monopoly.

Regards Dan, NORWAY.

Dear Santa Claus,

I hope you're fine, but I'm sure it'll be a long night Christmas Eve. Do you make the presents yourselves and deliver them to the houses? I have blue eyes and brown hair, and like football, computers, and reindeer – could you please send me a picture of them? I wish for a computer, but I've been a little bad this year, however will you forgive me? I hope you'll have a nice Christmas and remember to wear thick clothes so you'll keep warm.

Yours a hopeful Scott, ENGLAND.

Dear Santa Claus,

I ask you to please be kind and send me a Christmas card from your house. I hope I'll get a lot of surprises Christmas Eve. I promise too I'll be a very good girl.

Best regards from Banti, HUNGARY.

Dear Santa Claus,

I've tried to be nice, but it was difficult so it's OK if you don't give many presents. But please give me some, and then I'll make a plate of cookies and carrots for the reindeer. Remember that I'll put it on the floor next to the tree! The milk and the cookies for you I'll put on the table.

Your friend Christopher, USA

BEST WISHES FOR YOU

To: Santa Claus :

Hello! Are you still busy?
I really enjoy reading your letter and so I decided to write you again this year!

Year 2008 is a hard year for people around the world as the ~~free~~ economy really in "bad" situation. I hope all of us can cope with it and have a good Year ahead!

Best Wishes,
Shirley
'08 Winter

Thinking of you and wishing you all
the joys of this beautiful season.

To Santa,

Why didn't you come to me Christmas Eve? I got everything I wanted, but you didn't come. My big sister says that I wasn't nice enough, and that's why you didn't come. What do your pixies eat by the way? And where do they live? My big sister doesn't believe in pixies. Are they for real or are they just dressed up? Hope I receive an answer so I know that you exist.

Love Synne Marie, NORWAY.

Santa Claus,

I know that I haven't been nice this year, but I promise to be nice next year. So wouldn't it be alright to give me something in advance?

Regards Jose, SPAIN.

Hello dear Santa,

I wish you a merry Christmas and a happy New Year's Eve. Yes, I'll be good the entire 2004 if you answer me.

Your Holger, GERMANY.

In Morocco Santa Claus is known as "Black Peter"!

For Santa,

Thanks a lot for all the nice presents I've got from you. I've been a good boy this year, at least once in a while, so I hope you come here this year as well. I'm looking forward to Christmas which we're going to celebrate with my grandmother and grandfather. I wish for a new computer game, a sword, a toy mouse, and several sections for my train. Merry Christmas and a happy New Year.

Regards Krister, NORWAY.

Caro babo Claus,

Here's my wish list. I think I've been nice, but just in case you can ask my mum and dad.

Anizzolo, ITALY.

Dear Santa Claus,

I've been a good girl all year so please send me a present. I wish for apples or a red car. Could you by the way give me the address for another Santa Claus?

Regards Sakura, JAPAN.

Dear Santa,
I've been a good boy. I want the Lego airbase.
From Thomas, NORWAY.

Dear Santa,
Perhaps I haven't been very nice this year, but I'll put a bottle of Champagne and a bowl of chocolate eggs outside for you if I receive nice presents anyway.
Love Ashley, ENGLAND.

Hello Santa Claus,

I hope you are fine. Don't quiet, I won't forget to save carrots for your reindeer and I'll leave you many cookies and milk!
I like you because you deliver presents to all of the kids. I like you because you like milk and cookies and you always think of your reindeer!

Bye for now, Love Elise ...

Elise

DEAR SANTA

Dear Santa,

I was very nice on Birgitta's birthday and thus I at least
want you to give me my first wish. See wish list.

From Ejnar, SWEDEN.

P.S: We've moved to a bigger apartment right on top
of the old one. Same chimney!

Dear Santa,

I haven't been that good lately, but today I've
been good. I'll be good from now on if you bring
me Christmas presents.

Regards Petter, NORWAY.

In Greece, Santa Claus is known as Hagios Nikolaos.

Dear Santa,
Even though I haven't been the nicest kid, please
remember that I'm only a kid.
Regards, Kirsty, USA.

Dear Father Christmas.
My name is Frankie and I'm a good boy. I wish for a
present from you. Just a small one!
Grazie Frankie, ITALY.

Santa Claus,
I've been good all year and I'm planning to be good
next year as well. Thus, could you please quickly throw
a yo-yo into an envelope and send it to me?
Sebastian, POLAND.

Hallo Santa Claus,

How are you? I'm fine and have been good all year. So will you deliver me toys? I would also like to see the place you live. I look good, am kind, sometimes serious, I'm thin, intelligent, 10 years old and live in Mexico.

Love Patricia, MEXICO.

Dear Santa,

How would you define good and not good? Isn't it allowed to tease once in a while? I do have 4 siblings!

Best regards, Amy, ENGLAND.

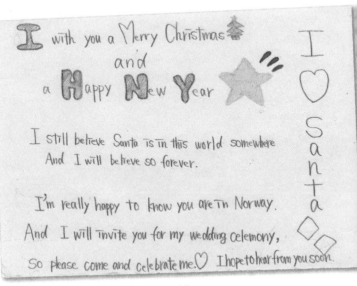

Dear Santa,

I'm at aunt Karin's this year. Please deliver my presents there after dinner. You're welcome to deliver some extra presents for me because I would like that since I've been so nice.

From Kikki, SWEDEN.

Dear Santa,

I promise to be a good boy, and I really want a punching ball, Free Willy video, Robin Hood book, and a new football. I'll give you a present and something for the reindeer. Many kisses!

Best regards James, ENGLAND.

Babbo Natale!

I want a battery car that can drive at least 10 km/h. Then I promise you that I'll be good at least until our summer vacation. Perhaps longer?

Sandro, ITALY.

DEAR SANTA

Dear Santa,

I'm a very good boy so please give me a lot of presents. Where do you live? If you come to Japan, I would like to talk to you. Why can reindeer fly in the sky? Where do you buy all the presents? Did you receive any presents when you were a child? What do you do on all the other days? How many reindeer do you have?

I would like a pair of nice shoes.

From Jo, JAPAN.

Dear Father Christmas,

I'm seven years old. Please give me a scooter.

I've actually been good all year.

From Amy, SOUTH AFRICA.

Hello Santa Claus,

My name is Cato. I'm very nice because I take care of my little brother. I also take care of my dog, and I help mum and I help dad. I wish for a new Playstation, Nintendo, Thomas the Tank Engine model train set, money, etc.

I hope you'll come to our house this year.

Best regards Cato, ITALY.

48

Hallo Weihnachtsmann

Na, wie geht es Dir? Ich hoffe mal gut
Mir geht es „supi"

Ich hoffe, dass meine Lehre gut läuft,
so dass ich Geld verdienen kann.
Ich möchte auch mein Hauptschulabschluss
schaffen und später einen Job bekommen.

Ich hoffe dass, Du mir Glück wünschst

Herzliche Grüße   und fröhliche
        Deine Nicob aus Rostock   Weihnachten

Hab Dich lieb

Dear Santa,

I hope you're fine, I can't say that I've been good all year, but at least half the time. If I had been nice all year, I probably would have got a full bag of presents from you. Now I only get half a bag. But when you see my wish list you'll find out that it's heavy stuff. Therefore I'm going to get everything I want anyway because you can't possible carry them in a full bag.

Best regards George, SCOTLAND.

Carissimo Babbo Natale,

I've been good to Andrea, at least this week, and remember that I was nice last summer too!

Love Gaia, ITALY.

BIRGER SIVERTSEN

Dear Santa Claus,

My name is Dessi and I'm 12 years old. I live in Sofia,
Bulgaria. I'm a very good student, and I promise to be a
kind child. I'll be happy if I get 100 dollars for
Christmas shopping from you. Thanks a lot!
Best regards Dessi, BULGARIA.

Dear Father Christmas,

For Christmas I would like to have: a chocolate factory,
Egyptian fairytales, some clothes, some earrings, a
hamster, some books, and many surprises. In order to get
some of these presents I'll try to be nice to my sister and
try to help around the house when I can. I hope you'll have
a nice Christmas and a happy New Year... I'm sure I will!
Love from Nadine, ENGLAND.

In Norway, Santa is called "Julenissen", and makes his way
down the chimney the night of December 24th. Christmas
calendars are usual, and children get a small present in these
every day from December 1st to December 24th.

9/12-08

MINE BØRN HAR SET JERES
TREKANTEDE SKILTE MED
JULEMANDEN △ HOS NOGLE
VENNER OG ØNSKER SIG
RIGTIG MEGET AT FÅ ET HVER
- TRE STK. - I JULEGAVE.
KAN DET MON LADE SIG GØRE?
SÅ VIL DE BLIVE MEGET GLADE.
JEG VEDLÆGGER PENGE.

VORES ADRESSE ER:

KAISER & HERMANN

1265 KØBENHAVN K
DANMARK

JEG HÅBER MEGET, AT DET KAN
LADE SIG GØRE - TAK!
    - Lise Kaiser

Santa,

I want a super ice cream machine. I'm a very nice and good boy, so it's alright, right?

From Espen, NORWAY.

Dear Santa,

I don't know if I've been nice so I'll let you decide. No matter what I wish for: CDs (preferably with quiet music), riding gloves (winter, summer), riding whip (black), games (all sorts), good friends, Barbie dolls, Barbie stuff and a lot more.

Love Marit, NORWAY.

Dear Santa,

My name is Karolina, and I'm 12 years old, I live in Lithuania and I've been nice this year. Santa Claus! I wish you a merry Christmas and a fine New Year! I hope you'll send me a present and that the reindeer will be able to carry it. I'll appreciate seeing you on Christmas Eve.

Best regards and love Karolina, LITHUANIA.

Dear Santa Claus,

I haven't been particularly nice this year, but I hope
you'll still spend a few presents on me. Here's a list:
1) I want you to know that I'm too big for Barbie dolls,
and that I don't play with them anymore.
2) I would like a short skirt with a matching top.
3) A necklace for Mimi. His neck is quite big, but you
probably already know that since you know
all kinds of things.
4) I don't really care what you give me as long
as we have a deal?
From Amy, HONG KONG.

Dear Santa,

Are you busy? We are. Today we went to a Christmas
party with presents for poor people. We've baked pepper
biscuits. Come inside and you can taste them. I've
been good almost the entire time and I want snow
for Christmas, Duplo plane, Lego motor, Lego
castle, a police kit and books.
Best regards Andreas, NORWAY.

Dear Santa,

For Christmas I would like a skateboard. I've been a good boy; I've done what mum and dad have told me.

Best regards Vetle, NORWAY.

Dear Santa,

If mum and dad have sent you a letter saying that I haven't been nice last year, it's true. But remember that I really put myself together two weeks ago. Perhaps for just a week.

Best regards Rich, USA.

Dear Santa,

Once in a while I've been nice, but on Christmas Eve I'm always nice. I want a Batman suit and a remote controlled crane.

Best regards Per Axel, SWEDEN.

Dear Santa,

Hope you come on Christmas Eve, because I've been damn good!

Regards Stein, NORWAY.

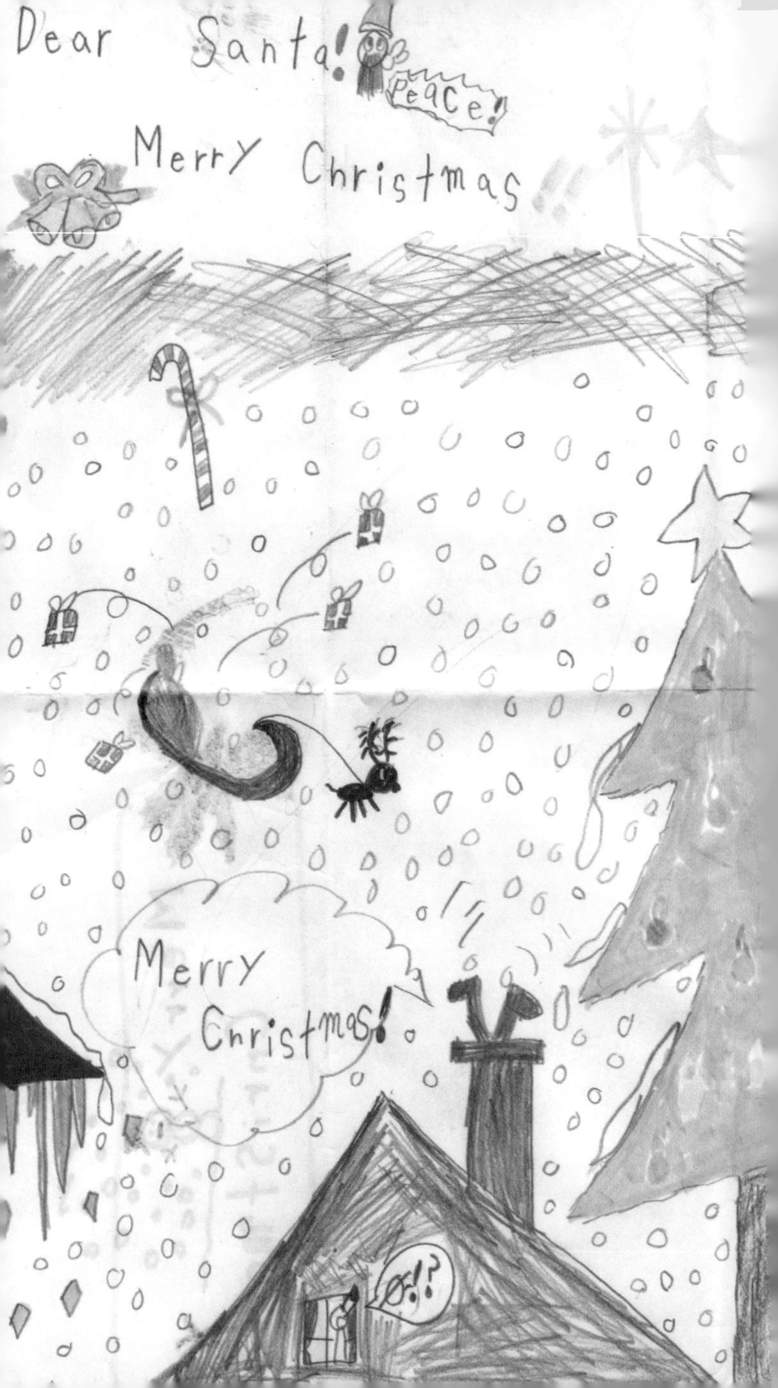
Dear Santa!
Peace!
Merry Christmas
Merry Christmas!

Dear Santa Claus,

If I get bunnies for Christmas and enough food to feed them, I promise to be nice to my sister all next year.

Best regards Keera, SCOTLAND.

Caro Babbo Natale,

I promise to help out in the stables next year, but I won't clean there because I'm afraid that the horses will kick me. Since I haven't been very nice this year, but promise to be nice next year, could I perhaps have the presents in advance?

Best wishes Micol, ITALY.

Dear Santa,

Sorry about this late letter, but mum has been working late waiting tables so we didn't have time before now. I hope you'll have a great Christmas Eve when all the presents have been delivered. I really just want snow for Christmas, but if you have time I would like to have a marble for the tree with my name on it. Have a great Christmas Eve, and remember that I've been really nice.

Best regards Caroline, NORWAY.

DEAR SANTA

Dear Santa,
I'm writing to you on behalf of my little sister
who's afraid to do it herself because she hasn't been that
nice this year. And it's true! She hopes that you'll
give her one or more presents anyway because
she promises to be nicer next year.
From Megan, ENGLAND.

Dear Santa Claus,
I've been so nice all year that a small present
just won't do, at least a clarinet!
Regards Aileen, GERMANY.

In the Netherlands Santa is known as "Sinter Klaas".
He rides a white horse, leaving gifts in wooden shoes.

Dear Santa...

Grown-ups and Santa Claus

Dear Santa Claus! Father Christmas.

My name is Julia Fedorova, I'm 26 years old, and I'm a maths teacher. I speak Russian, Ukrainian, and English. My English is not so good, I had a good teacher when I studied, but I wasn't a very good student, I write to you from Kiev, the capital of Ukraine. Perhaps you don't know where my country is. OK. Ukraine is a very big country. From west to east it's 1316 kilometers, and from north to south it's 893 kilometers. There are about 52 million people of different nationalities living here: Ukrainians, Russians, Jews, Moldavians, Poles, Hungarians, and Tartars etc. Christmas is a national holiday and is celebrated all over Ukraine. And it's an old tradition for Ukrainian people to celebrate New Years Eve twice: On the 1st and on the 14th of January. Now you know where I live. Father Christmas! A couple of days ago I opened the newspaper, found your address and wanted to write to you! Why? Because everybody believes in miracles. When I was a child I liked to read books with happy endings and liked to dream about nice stuff. And when I was older, I never stopped doing that either. Father Christmas! Please, please, please, give me and everybody I know and like a good health, fortune, love and mutual understanding, happiness and wealth. I want my wishes to come true. Please, help me! Father Christmas! You're a symbol of holidays and happiness, and I know that everything will be all right.

A lot of love, please write to me!

Kindly Fedorova, UKRAINE.

Letterina a Babbo Natale

caro Babbo... SE É POSSIBILE, PER NATALE IO VORREI:

IL CENTRO COMMERCIALE DI POLLY,

UN VIDEOGIOCO CHE SI CHIAMA STELLE SUL GHIACCIO,

E INFINE L'ABBONAMENTO ALLA PIMPA

GRAZIE

firma Fedeli Paola

DEAR SANTA

Mr. Santa Claus,

I want to become a good mother, I want my son to become the smartest guy in his school, and I want him to get accepted at Tamara High School. Please help us. I also hope that a world war will never happen again, and I hope that the war in Iraq will end soon, Thanks a lot!

From Chiyko, JAPAN.

Dear Santa Claus,

My name is Ada and I'm 31 years old. Please, give me my boyfriend back; let him come back to me. Many kisses from Athens, and a happy New Year.

Yours Ada (Antonia), GREECE.

My dearest Santa,

How are you? You're very busy now, right? I write to you every year, and you write back every time. Your letters are my treasures. You make me very happy, and you give me love, joy and dreams, I love you, Santa Claus! I'll visit your hamlet one day. These days I'm also quite busy because I have exams at Nursing School. I would like to become a nurse, you see, and I ask you to please pray for my success. And, if you can, write me some cheerful words. Perhaps that'll be my support for the rest of my life. I await your letter.

Love Akiko, JAPAN.

Dear Papa Nöel,

My name's Raguel, I'm 38 years old and live in Uruguay. I'm a teacher at school. Work with 23 boys and 10 girls. Last December I wrote to you, now I try again. I have a dream. To live in Norway for a while. I wish for photographs and books about your country. I love Norway! I like the high mountains, the blue rivers and you beautiful people. I need your letter.

1000 thanks and kisses for you.

Love Raguel, URUGUAY.

P.S: I'm sorry about my English; I speak Spanish!

15 12 05

menininhas

Para: Papai Noel

Eu gosto muito de você. Como é natal todas crianças pedem um brinquedo para você. Eu também quero pedir um brinquedo para você, mas agora vai ser você que vai escolher um brinquedo para mim. Eu sempre acreditei em você e nunca vou dixar de acreditar. Eu não ligo para o que os meus colegas falam? que você não existe mais eu sei que você existe, não se preculpe. Por favor escolha um brinque do que seja de barbie que eu goste muito.

Beijos !!!

Helena

Jilas do Atlântico-

Lauro de Freitas - Bahia - Brasil

CEP

tilibra

Hallo Santa Claus,

I'm from Belarus, and my name is Tatyana. The International Women's Day is March 8 every year, and is celebrated in Belarus, Russia etc, and it is a custom that men congratulate their girlfriends or wives, brothers congratulate their sisters, and children congratulate their mothers and grandmothers. I'm very fond of my mother, and wish to congratulate her. But I have a big problem. I don't have enough money to buy her a present. And the day is coming soon. Therefore I ask you, dear Santa Claus, for help. Hopefully you could be so kind as to send a small present or something soft, like a teddy bear. I want to say "thanks a lot" in an advance, dear Santa Claus.

With love, Tatyana White RUSSIA.

My dear Santa,

Happy New Year! It's very satisfactory to write to you. I hope to have such a good economy that I can visit you one day. May the New Year bring you happiness!

Yours Tomomi, JAPAN.

Dear Mr. Santa Claus,

I sincerely regret this late list of Christmas wishes and the inconveniences it may cause. However, I will strongly point out that I've been nice this year. Much nicer than usual, if I may say so myself. In those matters where there's doubt about my level of kindness, I want to point out that there has been either extenuating circumstances or that I wasn't in full possession of my faculties when committing the act. List of wishes:

1) Kjerstin, the most beautiful girl in the world, and whom I love more than anyone in the world.

2) A camel/dromedary (a stylish means of transportation and a good friend).

3) A minor nuclear bomb to hold a fashionable glass table (the nuclear bomb may be without explosives and plutonium if that can contribute to better working conditions for Santa and remove the problems getting hold of it, but I'm sure Santa has some good contacts)...

4) A house on the moon.

Yours sincerely Tore Johannes, NORWAY.

In Finland, Santa Claus is known as "Joulupukki".

BIRGER SIVERTSEN

Dear Santa,

Thanks for allowing us from Kenya to write to you.
I want to spend my Christmas vacation in Norway, and
I think I have enough money for a three months stay.
The main thing I want to ask you is regarding a visa
that I'm trying to get right now from the Norwegian
embassy. I've been told that I need somebody to
correspond with in Norway. This person must be willing
to sponsor me a plane ticket and pay for my hotel room.
Santa: I would like you to send me a letter containing:
Your name, fax number, telephone number, address etc.
I write you the name of my bank and bank account
number for my sponsor. Please, Santa, send me this and
God will bless you and me. I promise not to use a single
krone of your money; all I need is a guarantee so I can
get hold on a visa. The visa process will take two weeks.
I'll be happy if you can send me an answer as soon as
possible. Santa, please, if one of your friends or relatives
can give me this, or yourself, I'll be the happiest man on
earth. If I come to Norway I want to meet you, and I will
thank the sponsor personally. Once again, Santa Claus,
I thank you for answering us here in Kenya.
Greetings from Isaac, KENYA.

9.12.08

An den Weihnachtsmann !!

Lieber Weihnachtsmann,

hast du eigentlich auch einen Vornamen? In dem Buch „Als der Weihnachtsmann vom Himmel fiel" (Cornelia Funke) steht als Name: Niklas Julebukk. Oder hast du so viel Namen, wie du genannt wirst, dass du gar keinen richtigen Namen hast? So das alle Namen gelten?

Außerdem wünschte ich gern wissen, wo du wohnst. Ich will nämlich nicht, dass meine Post nach irgendwo anders hinkommt und dort von anderen gelesen wird. Wenn man z.B. nach Himmelpfort schreibt, bekommt man nie eine richtige Antwort.

Hast du wirklich so zwei kleine Englein und Kobolde, oder machst du alles allein? Jedenfalls hoffe ich, dass du nicht sehr viel Helfer hast, die deine Post lesen!
Bitte antworte mir.

* * * * * * * *

Außerdem wünsche ich mir, dass in unserer Familie alles schön bleibt und alle gesund sind und das du Wuschel (mein Meerschwein.) auch etwas mitbringen könntest. Vielleicht zum Klettern oder irgendetwas, über dass sie sich freut. *(falls das himmel ihn vielleicht nicht beeinflusst)*

und könntest du vielleicht für jeden (Mutti, Vati, mich, Isven) so eine kleine Weihnachtsüberraschung schreiben, über di jeder sich freut?

Du könntest uns auch bestimmt endlich besuchen, oder zumindest die Geschenke nicht nur abgeben, denn schließlich haben wir Hausschuhe oder du läufst einfach in Socken durch unsere Wohnung, damit der helle Teppich nicht schmutzig wird.
Du kannst deine Stiefel doch ausziehen, oder?

Ich würde mich sehr freuen, wenn du antwortest!

Julia

Dear Santa Claus,

I'm growing up now. Half way to 50. Can I still write you? I would still like a dog; big enough to drag me on ski rides, small enough to warm my feet in bed. There's one thing that has puzzled me for a while: Are you a Christian? I mean people die, get buried and – except for Jesus – they don't come back. But you come back every single Christmas without looking any older. Why is that? Do you have an eternal life? In that case I think many people wish for the same, or at least want to know what you do the rest of the year to keep in such good shape. Perhaps you're also a Santa for everybody who celebrates other holidays than the birth of Jesus. Santa Claus (or do you prefer Santa? What are you called in private?), we're many who send you letters and lists of all the things we wish for. Are you cooperating with mum or are you competitors? Under the tree there are so many presents which supposedly have been delivered by you, but only a few have a to- and from-card that says that it's actually from you. I'm confused about who actually gives me the presents. Do you get any presents? Mum always wanted nice children when I was little, even if she already had that. If I give you a piece of nice little me, would you give me a dog? Merry Christmas!

Sincerely Kristin, NORWAY.

PS: When you and the reindeer are out flying, do you meet a lot of jet planes?

DEAR SANTA

....

Dear Santa,

My biggest wish on earth is to get a car, or enough
money to buy one, before I get too old.
Regards Vivchenko, RUSSIA.

Dear Santa,

Perhaps I'm writing you a bit early, but the shops here are
full of Christmas stuff, pixies, pixy wives, stars, candles
etc. Don't know if you remember me from last year?
Sent you some Christmas wishes (I didn't get them),
but I'll try to send you a wish list again this year. May I
remind you that I can't afford anything! Merry
Christmas to you, dear Santa.

Cozy regards from Anne-Lise, NORWAY.

BIRGER SIVERTSEN

Dear best friend,
I received your letter today with much joy, and ran to the post office to send you this reply. I wish and hope that our friendship will last very long, and I can't stop reading your cozy postcard – I read it again and again. I'm so grateful for perhaps getting help from you. I want to visit you and your beautiful country, where I'll meet you and your family! But I need a visa to come to your country, and I can get it at your embassy in Tunis, Tunisia. So – could you send me the necessary papers I need in order to get the visa? Before I end this letter I wish to know everything about you; job, hobbies and everything about your small town.
Sincerely Redouatie, ALGIERS.

Santa Claus,
Please! I want a picture of Santa Claus for my daughter!
Kind regards Silvia, ITALY.

Dear Father Christmas,
This Christmas I want something special: A ticket that'll allow me to travel around the entire world. I hope you can make that wish come true!
Yours Maxime, FRANCE.

71

Dear Santa Claus,

I live in Czech Republic and I'm the mother of two girls aged six and three. Jerìsek (baby Jesus) gives away presents in Czech Republic. My children would like to write to him – give him their Christmas wishes, something I would like too. But he doesn't have a post office like you, and that's the reason I write to you. Could you, dear Santa, send presents to my children? They would be very happy. I also have a little request from you. I collect pens made of wood, and have a huge collection – but no Christmas pens. Do you have any pens with Santa Claus? I send you my warmest greetings, and I'm looking forward to hearing from you.

Yours Gabriella, CZECH REPUBLIC.

Dear Father Frost,

I read an article about you and decided to write a letter. My name is Irina, I'm 23 years old and live in Russia. I'm married and our son Vladik is six months old. I want him to have a happy and merry Christmas. If possible, I'll appreciate if you can send him a toy car. In advance, a thousand thanks, and we all wish you well in Christmas.

Yours Irina and family, RUSSIA.

Dear Father Christmas,

This year is marked by the fact that I've been working really hard, and therefore I think I deserve one or two extraordinary presents from you for the first time in my adult life. Here are my wishes:

1) A huge Mercedes four wheel drive.

2) A long vacation.

3) A new set of golf clubs.

4) New tennis equipment.

5) Ski vacation.

Sincerely Roger, SPAIN.

Mister Santa,

In connection with New Years I'm happy to write you this letter and tell you about myself. I have a good health, and I think a lot about you and your family. I wish you a happy new year, good health, happiness and peace. And Santa Claus; could you tell me about yourself and what you're going to do in the future, if you have any idea about that.

Regards Mr. Benabdellah, ALGIERS.

Dear Santa,

I'm planning a "trip around the world" and will appreciate meeting you. I'll get in touch when my traveling plans have been arranged.

Sincerely Emiko, JAPAN.

Dear Santa Claus,

Are you for real? I think you live in Finland in a house deep in the forest and have many animals. I'm happy when I think about you. I look forward to Christmas this year, take care!

From Etsuko, JAPAN.

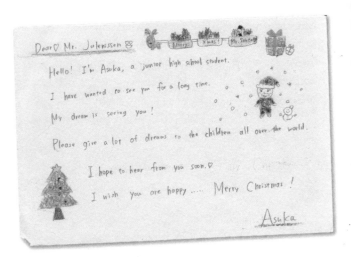

Dear ♡ Mr. Julenissen ♥♥

Hello! I'm Asuka, a junior high school student.

I have wanted to see you for a long time.

My dream is seeing you!

Please give a lot of dreams to the children all over the world.

I hope to hear from you soon. ♡

I wish you are happy ..... Merry Christmas!

Asuka

Dear Santa,

This is the first time I write to you. I've heard that I can't be sure to receive an answer from you. My name is Yasuyuki (...), and I live in Chiba, Japan. I'm a teacher in high school. Last spring I changed school, and it was here I met a woman who's also a teacher. The moment I met her I fell in love. I could have gotten married a long time ago, but I never met the ideal woman. When I saw this woman the first time I thought; "I finally met her. She is my ideal woman." I was eager to talk to her.

Sunday the 28th May I asked her if she wanted to eat lunch with me, and on the way back I told her about my feelings for her. Then she told me that she's in love with another man whom she wants to marry. More than seven months have gone since I met her the first time. And of course I can't forget about her. She makes me happy all the time. She makes me happy even when I'm sad. I think she knows that I still love her after all this time. I want to tell her about my thoughts. I want to tell her how much I love her, and how much she means to me. Even though she'll become a stranger's wife in the near future, I can't forget about her. I don't know what to do.

Therefore, dear Santa, please tell me what I'm supposed to do from now on. I'm looking forward to receiving a letter from you.

Sincerely Yasuyki, JAPAN.

Dear Santa Claus,

We discovered your address in an Italian magazine and decided to write this letter for you in English because we don't know the Norwegian language and you hardly know Italian. Recently, we've been wanting to believe in you the same way we did as kids. Next year, in 2004, we're getting married and would like a present from you – but preferably you blessing our life together. Unfortunately we don't have a place to live and live from day to day until we find an apartment near our works. We hope that our huge love for one another will conquer all problems. It's late now, it's 11:35 p.m., and we're going to bed like good children. We wish you a very merry Christmas and a happy New Year and the same to all children who have believed in you – or believe – because those who believe will have a future with you!

Ciao, Carlo and Sara, ITALY.

Dear Friend,
I thank you for many fine Christmases and years. For
dreams and health among other things. My son believes
that it's Santa Claus who gives away the presents
Christmas Eve. This year I'll tell him the secret and
give him the presents myself. Thanks a lot!
Sinji, JAPAN.

My dear Christmas friend,
I hope you're fine, and I wish you a merry Christmas
and happy New Years Eve. I hope this Christmas will
bring you happiness and joy in life. I don't know when
your birthday is, mine is April the 25th. You know that
I'm a poor man; I would like to be sponsored by you, and
ask you for a small video camera for Christmas.
Sometimes I consider traveling to Norway to look for
a job after I've finished my studies. Please accept me.
I ask you once again, politely and respectfully,
if you'll please send me a small video camera.
I hope that you're a gentleman.
Yours, S. Mahesh, INDIA.

Dear Santa Claus,
I'm really surprised that you exist in the world;
this is the first time I write to you. I want to write to
you every year. This year is also the first time I leave
my country to study in Australia. I would like to
send greetings to my grandmother and my boyfriend
because they helped me a lot. And I would like to have
a grey Lacoste t-shirt, size 3 (for women).
Regards Livian, AUSTRALIA.

Dear Santa Claus,

I'll appreciate knowing more about how Christmas is celebrated in Norway. I saw your address in a magazine that wrote about Christmas in Norway. In Zambia we also celebrate Christmas, and from the article I understand that we have many similarities. In Zambia we have several parks with wild animals that people are interested in seeing. If you're interested or if anybody else is interested, we can make a deal, and perhaps I can come and make an arrangement for you next Christmas in Norway. We also have the second largest national park in Africa, and the famous Victoria Falls which is a really neat place to see. If you want more information let me know, and I'm also interested in knowing more about Norway. I'll introduce myself: I'm married and have three kids, two boys and a girl. I would also like to have friends in Norway. I'll be very grateful if you answer my letter.

Yours Beatrice, ZAMBIA.

NB: If you and I start writing to one another, we'll exchange many interesting things.

In China, Santa Claus is known as "Shengdan Laoren".

Dear Santa,

Merry Christmas and
A happy New Year 2009!!

Sincerely you

JUNNA

Dear Santa,

My name is Natascha, and I write to you on behalf of
my younger brother Jack. He has great learning
disabilities and can't really talk. Now he can only write
a little bit; he's 8 and likes football and cars.
Sincerely Natascha, ENGLAND.

Dear Santa,

Hi, my name is Christos and I'm 31 years old. I would
like a baby! Merry Christmas and happy New Year.
Love Christos, GREECE.

Dear Mr. Santa Claus,

When I was a child I believed that you existed.
Now I'm not really sure. Do you exist?
If you really exist – write to me!
Sincerely Bobby, ENGLAND.

In the US and Canada, Santa is called Santa Claus.
He is also called "Kris Kringle" which comes from the
German term "the Christ Child".

DEAR SANTA

Dear Santa Claus,

I read an article about you in a local paper, and I'm interested in sending you a letter. You live in an area where there's snow so you need to wear a thick coat. That must be wonderful! I live in a tropical place without snow in the winter. Do you like living in such a cold place? Well, I would have like to have had some experiences with snow if had had the chance. One more thing. Do you need to travel around the world to deliver the presents? What countries do you go to, and what means of transportation do you use? I would like to know a lot of things, and I'm grateful if you answer my many questions. Looking forward to receiving a letter from you.

Yours, Anne, CHINA.

Dear Santa Claus,

I write to you because I have a small problem. I have a daughter who no longer believes that you exist because her teacher has told her that those who believe in you are old fashioned people. My daughter is 8 and I'll be forever grateful if you'll write her a letter so she regains her faith in Santa Claus. A thousand thanks!

Sincerely Lara, ITALY.

Dear Santa Claus,

I'm sure you're extremely busy lately. When do you plan to begin your trip around the world? And – how well are your reindeer? I hope you're well and I enclose a Japanese stamp as a present for you. The tree in the picture is very famous for its old age and its wonderful flowers, and it is situated in Fifu. Every year in April many people come to see it. When you fly over Japan you'll most likely be able to see it.

Yours Kohta, JAPAN.

Dear. Mr. Julenissen

I'm Mika, a junior high school student in Japan. I have questions for you. How old are you? I'm fifteen years old. Can raindeers fly? I think they can fly.

Can you make masics? I think you can. Wishing you all the best in 2009. I wish for peace Merry Christmas.

Dear Santa,

For 30 years I haven't written a letter to Santa Claus because I didn't believe that he existed. Now I found the address on the Internet, and I give him a chance to prove that there's a Santa in the world – if he writes me back. My name is Tsuiyin, and I have been a kind and good child throughout all these years. I hope that my wish comes true, and wish you a merry Christmas and a Happy New Year!
Sincerely Tsuiyin, USA.

Dear Santa,

Thanks a lot for answering my letter. That made me very happy, and I hardly believed it. I don't know if you've received a letter from Indonesia before – if my letter was the first, I feel like a very happy person. And thank you for giving me and my family a great Christmas last year. This year I want my family to be able to spend Christmas with a lovely tree inside the house, something we haven't had for many years. And I want the new year to bring me a good job because I want to be able to help my parents so the family can have what they want. One day I would like to visit you and your reindeer. I wish you a merry Christmas, I'm so happy today, Santa! Do you want to visit me on December 24th?
With love from Rieke, INDONESIA.

Dear Santa Claus,

First of all I'm writing you this letter to wish you a merry Christmas. And I'll be very grateful for every present I get from you. I know that you're really busy, but I truly hope that you'll find time to answer me. If you respond my friend Brian will be convinced that you exist – and live in Norway.

Yours Sandra, ENGLAND.

Dear Santa Claus,

1,000 thanks for the nice apartment we got right before Christmas. I bet you had something to do with that. If mums are allowed to wish for something too, I wish for good grades (A) for my thesis and oral exam, and a fun job that pays well.

Hugs from Hanne, NORWAY.

P.S: We've moved, as you know, and Peter says that we can probably use the new stairs on Christmas Eve. If not, you'll have to use the basement entrance and walk up to the second floor.

In Sweden, Santa is called "Jultomen", and visits the evening before Christmas Day, pulling a big bag of "Julklappar" (Christmas presents) in the deep snow.

Dear Santa

Hello. I'm Natsumi
I'm from Japan. I like music.
I like Ashley Tisdaie.
My sister likes dogs.
I am a junior high school
student. My birthday is July
15. I have many friends.

See you on the christmas
Day!

Sincerely yours,
by Natsumi

Dear Santa Claus,

I'm a 31 years old Italian girl who really needs a present. I would like to have 25.000 Euro to buy an apartment. If you're able to help me, I'll appreciate very much.

Love Susi, ITALY.

Dear Santa,

I write you this letter after having read "Christmas in Norway". I'm from Ethiopia, but now live in Nairobi, Kenya. My interest in learning more about your country came after a delegation from your country allowed me to live in Norway. I understand that Droebak is a Christian town so I wonder if it's possible to settle down there or in the nearby areas?

Your brother Abe, ETHIOPIA/KENYA.

Dear Santa Claus,

I got hold of a book at the Norwegian consulate in which I found your address. Could you please send my father a letter? He'll be thrilled to receive a letter from you, from Norway. His family was from Lillehammer in Norway.

Kind regards from Rachel, USA.

Dear Santa,

Some tell me that you live in Finland, but I don't believe in that information. I think you're in Norway right now. As far as I'm concerned both Santa Claus and MadDonald are respectable people because they often give several presents to children all over the world. And soon Christmas will arrive. Therefore I hope that my little friends and I will receive something from you. It would be neat if you could send us each a present, if possible. We would thank you very much!

Sincerely Huang, CHINA.

P.S: Enclosed are our names and addresses. They're all my friends, please give them some presents for a happy Christmas.

Dear Santa Claus,

I write to learn more about your service to people in Norway and other countries. Christmas must be the busiest season for you. Please tell me about yourself and your work. I wish you a fine Christmas and a happy New Year.

Yours Vahid, IRAN.

Dear Mr. Santa Claus,
Please really enjoy your summer vacation.
Love Nao, JAPAN.

Dear Father Christmas,
I invite you or anybody in your family to come and visit us.
Your friend Michael, TANZANIA.

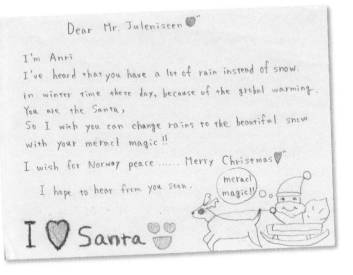

DEAR SANTA

Dear Santa Claus,

I'm too old for a present, but I'm a huge stamp collector.
In my entire life this is the first time I write to you.
I wish you a merry Christmas, and put a bit of peace
in the envelope. And oxygen too.

Yours Poletti, ITALY.

Dear Santa Claus,

This is a greeting from Beijing (Peking), China. Maybe
this letter arrives late for Christmas and New Years, but
I still hope that you'll accept my greeting. Here in Beijing
the weather is alright, a little cold and not much wind.
I presume that it's much colder in Norway. I think
Christmas must be the biggest festival in Norway
throughout times, and that it's the time where you're most
busy delivering presents to children all over the world.
I work in DHL and have been told that the real Santa lives
in Norway due to fast delivery. Perhaps you also
distribute presents trough DHL Express? You don't have to
write me if you're busy, but if you do, I'll be very flattered!
I hope you be well and happy for the rest of the year.

Best regards Jia, CHINA.

PS: Send me an email if that's easier for you.

90

Dear Santa...

Teachers and Santa Claus

Dear Mr. Santa,

I'm a teacher in Japan. Enclosed you'll find 100 letters that my students have written. Maybe some of the letters are hard to understand because some of the students have just started learning the language. My older students have more experience. I realize that it takes a lot of time and many difficulties answering all the letters, but the children are very hopeful. If time's a problem for you, don't hesitate to write a standard letter in which you change the names. And please send the letters to their home addresses. If you have any problems with the addresses, please send the letters to me to the address above mentioned. I appreciate the time and care you spend making a special Christmas for every child in the world. Peace and love for you and your dear ones.

From Ayako, JAPAN.

Dear Santa Claus,

I'm a teacher in 1. grade. My 21 pupils are 6 and 7 years old. It would be a great pleasure for them to receive a letter from Santa Claus. Since I don't know if you speak German, I also write some words in English because I think you speak English more often in Norway. I'm a teacher. The pupils are 6 and 7 years old. Will you write to them?

Best regards Sigrid, GERMANY.

Dear Papà Nöel,

My name is Raquel and I live in Libertad, Uruguay, I'm 37 and a teacher. I wish you a merry Christmas and a happy new Year. I'm sorry about my English, but I actually speak Spanish. Kisses for you.

Raquel, URUGUAY.

Dear Santa Claus,

Hello, my name is Kelko. I'm 37 years old. I teach the students English. I send you a bunch of letters that the kids have written in school. I would like you to give me a talent for teaching. I hope my students will be able to learn to write to you in English one day.

Merry Christmas!

Sincerely, Kelko, JAPAN.

Lieber Nikolaus,
ich heiße Nico und bin 9
Jahre alt. Mein Heimatort
ist Halle in Deutschland.
Ich habe eine Frage:
Wann kommst du?
Mein größter Wunsch
ist ein Spiel "Messing".
Viele Grüße d dein
Nico.

Dear Santa Claus,

We, girls and boys in this school, decided to write to you after seeing an article about you in the newspaper. There was your address. So we decided to write you a letter and ask for your help. We would appreciate it if you send us some Christmas candy. Perhaps you are very busy, but please Santa, send us a letter. Some people don't believe that you are real, but they're lying to us. Because we know that you live in Norway where you have your factory and your helper-assistants, and you have a wonderful magic. We are: 10 girls and 8 boys who send you Christmas wish lists and best wishes for the New Year. Good luck!

With love, your Bulgarian friends.

PS: Dear Santa Claus! My name is Svetlana. I'm a teacher and headmaster of this boys and girls. They really wanted to write to you and receive presents. And I on my behalf would like to ask you if you'll give my 13 year old son a pair of skis for Christmas. It's very difficult for me to buy skis. He likes winter and skiing, and it's is necessary for his physical training. I wish you happiness and good health.

Your Svetlana, BULGARIA.

In England, Santa is called "Father Christmas", and has a very long beard and a long coat.

95

Nov 17 2008

Dear Santa
Hello I'm Mai
I'm from Japan.
I am a junior high school student.
I study English.
I like piano very much.
How about you?
I would like to want a teddy bear.
I have many fri

See you on
the
Christmas
Day!

Sincerely yours
Mai!

Dear Santa Claus,

First of all I wish you a merry Christmas, and then I must say that I believe in you. I hope there will be peace in the world soon, and I wish you can make everybody happy. I'm very happy at Christmas and last Christmas I had a good time with my friends. This year I have a boyfriend for the first time, and I hope to spend a nice Christmas with him. I ask you to be so kind and give me a wonderful Christmas! I graduated last year, and now I'm a teacher in a school. I work very hard, but it's not always easy. Finally, I wish for good health to my family. Take care and thank you for reading my letter.

Your Akiko, JAPAN.

Lieber Santa,

I'm a teacher in Germany whose theme these days is to write letters, and I've found out that they should write to you. First of all: I understand that your name is Nicholaus, Santa in Norway, and I must say it's a very nice name. Naturally I have some questions for you: How's the weather in Norway at this time of year? Is it snowing as in Germany? Does it get dark early? I wish you a fine Christmas and I'm looking forward to hearing from you.

Your Anja, GERMANY.

Dear Santa,

Long time no see! Where have you been? It's been a year since I wrote to you. My name is Eiichi and I'm an English teacher in a high school in Tokyo. Every single November I've considered teaching my students how to write you a letter in English. I know you have a lot to do at winter time, and I know that you're very busy, but please receive their letters and write them back. Take care!

Kind regards Eiichi, JAPAN.

Not only teachers, but also headteachers write letters to Santa Claus. Since 1996 a very well-known Japanese headteacher (Prof. Dr.) with many contacts has sent a long letter to Santa Claus every year. In the letter he includes all the important things that have happened to him during the year, both private and work-related. Several top politicians, managers, known professors and public people would be surprised to learn that their visits have been reported to Santa Claus. The headteacher always encloses several pictures that prove these visits and other events that he wants to show to Santa. He always concludes his letter by giving Santa a warm invitation to come and visit, and in the end he writes: "Our guestroom is always ready for you, and we hope to see you soon".

Dear Santa...

Questions
for Santa

Dear Santa,

Hallo. This is the first time I write to you. My name is Fumie, and I'm a 16 year old girl who's a high school student in Japan. I know that you really live in Christmas Land. It said so in a brochure that was given to me last summer. I can't express myself well enough in English to say what I wish to say so I'm looking up the words I don't know in my English dictionary. Good heavens! It's fall in Japan now. The leaves on the trees have started to turn red and yellow. Soon winter will come, and I'm looking forward to hearing the voice of December that gives us Christmas. Christmas is also celebrated in Japan. We exchange presents and cards, and I would like to exchange cards with you this year. I have some questions for you: How old are you? I presume that you're very old? Do you get up early this season? You must be really busy writing cards.

Regards from Fumie, JAPAN.

Dear Santa,

I guess you have a lot to do before Christmas. Hope you have time to come and visit me Christmas Eve. Is it OK to come to grandma's in Vestre Noesegate instead of our house?

Regards Silje, NORWAY.

Babbo Natale,
Are you really that chubby?
Regards Mario, ITALY.

Dear Santa,
How do you manage to climb down so many chimneys
and be in so many places around the world in just one
night? I would like to have books and computer games
for Christmas, and I promise to continue being a nice
boy, Santa, it's alright if I don't get what I wish for.
It's OK, but try to do your best.
Kiss from Ivo, BULGARIA.

Dear, Nisse! (Jake Frost) Russia

I have not friend. I am friendless woman.

I would like get to know with man. It is my wish.

I am simple, modest, polite woman. I would like to be with man as like as me.

I am 61 age. My height - 1m 60 cm. My weight - 52 kg. I don't drink alcohol. I don't smoke. I have one son. He is 38 age. He is alone as like as me. I am pensioner now. Howerer I have my young, kindly soul.

Dear, Nisse, please, help me. I know English and Russian languages only.

I hope hear from you soon as you can. Before thank you.

I wish you health.

Your sincerely Luda

Dear Santa Claus,

How are you? My name is Charlie and I'm nine years old. I like to play football and live in Hong Kong with my parents and sister. I'm a boy, I'm helpful and kind. How old are you? Do you like sports? Do you have a sister?

Your friend Charlie, HONG KONG.

Dear Santa,

What language do you speak? Is there perhaps something called North Polish since you live on the North Pole?

From Igor, RUSSIA.

Dear Santa,

How many employees do you have working in production?

Greetings from Matteo, ITALY.

Dear Santa Claus,

Do you think Arsenal is going to win a lot this season? Too much, perhaps?

Love Pablo, SPAIN.

Dear Santa Claus,
Why did you give Richard a Playstation 2 and not me?
Do you think that's fair?
Ted, USA.

🎅 🎅 🎅

Dear Santa,
Would you send me a little snow? Can you do that?
Love William, HONG KONG.

Dear Mr. Julehissen

I'm Naoya, a junior high school student in Japan.
I'm fifteen years old. I like a cat.
I can talk with a cat. I hope to hear from you soon!

I wish you a Merry Christmas
and
a Happy New Year.

辻 直也

Dear Santa,

Now it's finally Christmas again! Hope you're well in Korva Tinturi (pixie land) on the North Pole! I just want to ask you some questions. Do you know all the other Santas in other countries or do you deliver all the presents? I assume that you can't be the Italian La Befana or the Dutch Sinter Clas. On the 6th of December Sinter Clas will deliver presents so say hi to him from me when he's leaving to hand out fun and presents. Hope you can make everybody in the world who deserves it happy. I only wish for three things, and that's a portable computer, money, and books. I'm going to celebrate Christmas in Haugesund, right by the Vard mountain, and there's plenty of good things for your reindeer to eat in the mountains. Good wishes for a merry Christmas from me.

From Knut, NORWAY.

Dear Father Christmas,

Can you come and play tennis with my granddad?

Your Wataru, JAPAN.

Dear Santa.

Is it possible to get a list of what you have in store?

From Ian, SCOTLAND.

Dear Santa,

You're welcome to come and eat with me soon. And bring Rudolph. What are you giving Rudolph for Christmas? And who gives you presents? What kind of meat do you like best? And did you make a lot of money on the Coca Cola commercial last year? How many reindeer do you have? I'm also wondering if you have any other addresses for other Santas, preferably in the US? I think that perhaps Santa is an overweight American who digs MacDonald food and Coca Cola, with plenty of white hair and a long beard. Hair transplant is not impossible. Because it must be rather hot in the summertime. I hope that read this letter and forward it to the real Santa Claus.

Love Elisabeth, NORWAY.

Caro Babbo Natale,

How high do you fly when you have to cross the oceans? Do you ever lose some presents when you turn too fast?

Kindly Igor, ITALY.

In France, Santa Claus is known as "Pere Noel".

Dear Santa Claus,
How old is Rudolph and all the other reindeer? Have
you always had them, or are they children of the
old Rudolph or some of his fathers? Is Rudolph
perhaps your tenth Rudolph?
From Sofia, BELGIUM.

To Santa,
When you're finished with your job, could I perhaps
become the new Santa?
Your friend Callum, ENGLAND.

Hello, Santa Claus.
My name is Artyom.
How are you? I am 11 years old
I'm a pupil of the fifth form I live
In Russia, in zlakovo It is a town
on the rive Volga. Our town is not big,
but it is nice. I love my town and my country.
I have many friends I go in for football for two years.
Please give me a football ball
All the best.
Love
Artyom

Dear Santa,
How old are you? Have you reached 100?
From Alan, USA.

Cher Père Noël,
Why is it only you who go out in the world and
deliver presents? Why doesn't your wife help?
Is she afraid of heights, perhaps?
Love Rémi, BELGIUM.

Dear Santa,
Why don't I get a VCR?
Bartoss, POLAND.

Dear Santa Claus,
Could you tell me if it's fun to be Santa Claus?
What experiences have you had?
From Phoebe, TAIWAN.

Dear Santa,
Are we only supposed to wish for presents that we can use, such as games, Lego, clothes and so on?
Or can we wish for something else? I wish to remain 12 years old for the rest of my life if possible.
From Dan, POLAND.

Caro Babbo Natale,
Do you land vertically, like a helicopter?
Love Lorenzo, ITALY.

Dear Santa,
Do I get any of presents that I wish for?
Yours Zuzana, SLOVAKIA.

Cher Père Noël,
Can you send me a life sign before I send you my wish list?
From Gabriel, FRANCE.

Caro Babbo Natale,
Do you have teeth like regular people?
Who makes your glasses?
Yours Monica, ITALY.

Dear Santa,
Is there any chance that you'll switch to
a jet plane in the near future? And if so, what
type of plane will you prefer?
Love Zac, USA

Dear Santa,
I get about 20 Christmas presents every year.
It's not that much I think, do you realise that yourself?
When you come, you can count the presents
first, is that okay?
From Dennis, ENGLAND.

Caro Babbo Natale,
Is it too much to ask for a Game Boy?
Love Nicolo, ITALY.

Dear Santa,

I really need your help. I enclose a Christmas wish list from my dad, mum, sister, and baby brother, and if we receive all this will be a good Christmas for the entire family. Don't forget that I have a small present for you too when you arrive. I have a question for you: is it true that Christmas was cancelled for a couple of years in the seventeenth century by Oliver Cromwell?

Love from Benedict, ENGLAND.

Dear Santa Claus,

Mum and dad say that you won't come if I swear, is that true? If so, why are you allergic to swearing?

Regards Wictor, BULGARIA.

Hello Santa,

Do you enjoy it when you fly with the magic reindeer? Christmas greetings from Victoria, NORWAY.

Dear Santa Claus,

Will you bring me the presents I wish for this year?
Last year you disappointed me, and I didn't ask for that
much. If you disappoint me this year as well, I'll lock the
door so you can't let any more Christmases in.

From Martyna, POLAND.

Dear Santa,

Are you the Santa of Europe, while another one takes
care of the rest of the world (if so, where does he live) or
are there several? Are Father Christmas and Santa Claus
the same, or do they compete?

Love Tina, SWEDEN.

Dear Santa,

Don't you think that it is unfair that you give
away such fine and expensive presents but all you
get in return is something to drink and a little
food when you arrive?

Yours Agnes, POLAND.

Letterina a Babbo Natale

caro Babbo... SE È POSSIBILE, PER NATALE IO VORREI:

IL CENTRO COMMERCIALE DI POLLY,

UN VIDEOGIOCO CHE SI CHIAMA STELLE SUL GHIACCIO,

E INFINE L'ABBONAMENTO ALLA PIMPA.

GRAZIE

firma Jedeli Paola

DEAR SANTA

Dear Babbo Natale,

Ciao! Is it true that you wear Ray Ban sunglasses with yellow glasses in them when you're out flying?

Love Rebecca, ITALY.

Dear Santa Claus,

Is it because of all the times zones in the world that you manage to deliver presents to all the children? Or do you deliver on other days some places in the world?

From Konstantin, GREECE.

Dear Santa Claus,

Can we children come to your house and get the presents so we can see how you're doing? And what's your exact address, is it far away? Can we take the train or the bus, or do we need to be driven?

Greetings from Emilie, NORWAY.

Dear Santa Claus,

Could you call me when you're close by so I can come and say hello to you and reindeer? If you're busy I can call you after dinner. What's your cell phone number?

Love Rhiannon, SCOTLAND.

Dear you,
You do come to Poland this year again, right?
From Monica, POLAND.

Caro Babbo Natale,
What do you eat for dinner? What's your favorite food?
Do you like chilli peppers?
Love Martina, ITALY.

Cher Père Noël,
How often do you have to go back to the North Pole
to get more presents? I assume that you fly faster than
the speed of sound in order to get everything done in one
night, but still you don't get everything done, could
you tell me the name of your helpers?
Greetings from Jean-Paul, FRANCE.

Care Babbo Natale,
Have you watched Matrix Revolution?
Do you have such powers?
From Henry, ITALY.

Dear Santa Claus,

I don't know why you live so far up north. Why not in the Canary Islands where there is warmer? And how do you manage to stay so chubby? In all the movies I have seen I've never seen a shop; perhaps there is a hidden shop under the snow? Anyway this is the first time I write to you, so I truly hope that some of my wishes will come true. Christmas wish list:

1) Peace on Earth.

2) Equal food distribution to all countries.

3) Is it possible that I can receive a sign whether or not there is only life on our planet?

4) That HIV/AIDS epidemic will be erased.

By the way what do you do the rest of year? Because it is your helpers who make the presents, so perhaps you hibernate during the rest of the year? Everybody says you don't exist, but I don't believe that. I'm 15 years old and I believe in you, even though all the Christmas presents are carried from the bedroom by mum and out to the living room and placed under the Christmas tree. And we buy the presents ourselves. I wonder if I have ever seen you? Or are you just a fantasy figure that children are supposed to believe in until they grow out of it? Or are you a real person that really comes with presents Christmas Eve? I would like to see you perform live! Do you know that there are many who try to imitate you? They stand on corners and yell "ho ho" and beg for money? They are some awful wannabes! I hope you're a decent person who doesn't just receive letters from

children, reads them and throws them into the bin.
There are actually many, and I mean many, who believe
in you. Merry Christmas Santa Claus, you're
doing a great job.
Hugs from Ragnhild, NORWAY.

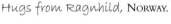

Dear Santa,
I've moved from Cumbria and I want you to have my
new address. Granddad has bought me a shiny pixie to
put in my window so you don't miss our new house
when you're in our neighborhood. Would you be so
kind and write me back so I know that you
got my new address.
Love Molly, ENGLAND.

Dear Santa,
Could you shave this Christmas so you can see what
you really look like under the beard?
Thank you in advance.
Love Ute, GERMANY.

Dear Santa Claus,

My brother believes that you must fly faster than a jet plane to reach everybody on Christmas Eve. How do you manage to stay on the sledge?

Love Martyna, POLAND.

Granarolo E., 1st December 2008

Dear Santa Claus,

My name is Nicholas and I am seven years old.

I live in Granarolo dell'Emilia which is a little village near Bologna in the North of Italy.

I started the second year at the local Elementary School last September, but though teachers say that I am good, I am always very frightened of making ... mistakes!!! .. Tell me, Santa Claus, did you also make mistakes when you went to school????

I have got a brother who is fourteen. His name is Andrea and he is also a bit .... naughty!!!

... He always tells me that you do not exist, but I do not believe him so I want to show his that .. he is wrong!!!

For this reason, I would like to ask you a very big favour:

.... could you please kindly send me a little postcard of Yours, so I could show Andrea that you ... really EXIST !!??!

I know I am a little bit cheeky, too ....

But I really promise I will try to do my best to be good!!!

I really look forward to receiving your kind special reply and ...

.... I thank you very much in advance !!!!

My family and I really wish you and your helpers

A VERY MERRY CHRISTMAS

And

A HAPPY 2009 !!!

Love,

Nicholas

Dear Santa,

I'd like a surprise for Christmas, but first I need to know
if you have any Christmas presents left?
Regards Shane, IRELAND.

Dear Santa Claus,
Is it true that you smoke a pipe?
From Erika, JAPAN.

Santa,

Could you hide a present in the living room that we
can look for on Christmas Eve?
Best Regards Daniel, SWEDEN.

Dear Santa Claus,

My name is Marco and I live with my mom and dad in
Barlassina near Milan in Italy. I wish to have a ticket to
a good Christmas and a happy New Year for my family
and for myself. You can fix that right? We thank you
and send you many kisses.
Goodbye Marco, ITALY.

DEAR SANTA

Hello Santa Claus,
I'm a member of a Judo club and I like to eat and read
books. Do you like Judo? Are you also a graduate?
From Kotomi, JAPAN.

Cher Papa Noël,
What does you sledge look like? Is it the same
that you always had or do you change it once in a
while? Does it have wheels? How big is it (number
of seats and trunk space)?
Yours Morgane, FRANCE.

Dear Santa,
I wished to have a pirate ship and a pirate in
a rowing boat last year. Do you remember? I didn't get
it, but Martin in my class did. Where those actually
my presents? This year I wish the same, don't mix
up the address this time!
Love Sindre, NORWAY.

Lieber Weihnachtsmann!
Wir sind zwei Brüder,
Ich bin ROBIN UND

mein kleiner Bruder
heißt Jon.
Wir würden uns riesig über
Post von Dir freuen,
denn dann wissen wir,
daß Du uns nicht

vergessen hast.

ROBIN

Liebe Grüße
ROBIN und Jon

Dear Santa Claus,
Do you wear snow goggles when you're sitting
in the sledge?
Love Monica, POLAND.

Dear Santa Claus,
Is there more for you to do every Christmas? In that
case you should hire more people every year. What
time of the year do you do that?
Love Tsunoda, TAIWAN.

Dear Santa Claus,
What do you sit on when you're traveling?
Not the reindeer, right?!
Regards, Alex, ENGLAND.

Care Babbo Natale,
Can I please have your autograph when you come here?
Yours Zilio, ITALY.

Dear Santa Claus,
How long does it take to drive from Norway to Japan?
What do you eat for lunch?
Best wishes, Misa, **JAPAN**.

Dear Santa,
Could you send me postcard,
I've heard so much about you.
Malvin, **NORWAY**.

Cher Père Noël,
Do you pay your workers well or badly? How
many hours do they work every day? Do they
get some days off once in while?
Love Angelique, **FRANCE**.

Dear Santa,
I hope that you'll come to us on Christmas Eve,
and I hope you have nice eyes. Do you?
Love Hanna and Mari, **NORWAY**.

Dear my Santa B,

Hello. My name is Junko and I am a Japanese girl. I have many questions for you. First! How old are you? More than 50? Next: do you have a wife? I know that you exist because I read it in an appendix of a magazine, that's the reason I am sending you this message. Of course I haven't been in Norway, so to my great disappointment I don't know much about your country. Please tell me about your country. Are there reindeer that pull sledges? In Japan we don't have reindeer. By the way I am 16 years old and in the second year of high school. Japan children have few dreams, I think. Japan is often called and "academic society". Everybody think about how high an academic degree they can have. How is it with the Norwegian people? Do many children have dreams of their own? I wish to visit Norway one day. Finally dear Santa, if you really read my letter I'll be very happy. I like English very much. But perhaps this letter has a lot of errors, then I become very sad. I'll wait for a letter from you. Adieu!

Sincerely Junko, JAPAN.

Dear Santa,
Will there be snow tomorrow or the day after or next week?
Love Elias, NORWAY.

DEAR SANTA

Care Babbo Natale,
I hardly had time to write you a Christmas wish list.
Then I thought about calling you. But you're not listed.
Could you please put your name and phone number in
the phone book so I can call you next time?
Yours Zanellato, ITALY.

Dear Santa Claus,
Do you like bananas?
Love Hoshito, JAPAN.

Hello Santa,
Could you send me the address for
Pippi Long Stockings?
Best wishes, Victoria, GERMANY.

Santa Claus,
How often do you change clothes?
Regards Tom, BELGIUM.

Dear You,

How do you manage to hide in the sky so nobody sees you? Isn't it scary with the planes around you?

Sincerely, Daniella, ENGLAND.

Caro Babbo Natale,

If I get all the presents I want, you'll get a lot of red wine when you come. Which wine do you prefer? Perhaps you like white wine better?

Love Pozzoli, ITALY.

To Santa,

Are you doing fine where you live? Do you have a lot of children there? Do you have candy for the children? Do you have a shop so you can buy food and sausages with ketchup and mustard? Do you have Mother Christmas with you? Do you have a swimming pool? Do you, dear Santa, want to come and visit us? That would be great, and we have both coffee and tea for you.

Best wishes, Rebecca, NORWAY.

Dear Santa Claus,
What do you say when you need to stop the reindeer
and when you start? Do you need to shout?
Hugs from Zuzia, POLAND.

For Santa Claus,
Mom and dad say that it's only nice kids who
get presents from you. But do you have
anything to do with Jesus?
Love Marcus, SWEDEN.

Dear Santa,
Do you know me, or is my name just on a list?
Regards Sabrina, GERMANY.

Dear Santa Claus,
When I see you on TV in foreign programs you are not
Japanese, but you are here. I know that you live on the
North Pole by Norway, but only Sami people live there.
Dear Santa. Are you Japanese, Westerner or a Sami?
From Nakano, JAPAN.

Dear Santa,

I've heard that you don't exist! So I'm writing you a letter to find out. I also wonder why you don't show up on Christmas Eve? Or perhaps it isn't you who comes? Do you only make the presents? Write back!

Greetings from Anne Viktoria, NORWAY.

01.12.2008

To: Santa Claus
     Julenissens Postkontor
     Torget 4
     1440 Drobak
     Norway

Hello Mr. Santa Claus,

my name is Stefan and im from Germany.

I hope everthing is okay with you?

Im looking forward to see you this year.
Please bring some presents, peace and a lot of snow on Christmas :-)

I wish you a mery Christmas, a happy new Year and a stress-free time!

I hope you write back!

bye
Stefan *Stefan*

Stef

DEAR SANTA

Dear Santa Claus,
Could you tell me what you did during the last world
war? You didn't fly around the world, that's for sure!
Where there any presents then?
From Andy, USA.

Dear Santa,
Can I sit next to you on the sledge when you fly?
I only need to sit there until we reach the neighbor
across the street, that's my aunt's house.
Best wishes Peter, HUNGARY.

Dear Mr. Santa,
How old are you? Why do you only wear
red and white clothes?
Love Mika, JAPAN.

Dear Santa Claus,
How often do you take a bath?
From Elisabeth, AUSTRIA.

Dear Santa Claus,

I hope you have Rudolph steering the sledge so you don't crash. What are the names of your favorite reindeer? Could I please have my VCR soon? I hope my step-sister will be able to come for Christmas so we can celebrate Jesus' birthday together. What colour is your underwear by the way? Do you and the Mrs. celebrate Christmas too? Last question: do you celebrate other holidays and do you have any children?

Merry Christmas and have a nice and safe trip!

Yours Rachael, USA.

Dear Santa Claus,

We go to kindergarten in Taiwan. Could you send us a picture of you? We have a question: What do you do when it's not Christmas? We like Christmases very much! God bless you!

Love from us in TAIWAN.

To Santa,

My name is Janne and I have a sister called Linn, but she's only 5 years old. We have written our wish list. But I have question for you. Did you come from the basement or from the attic last year? Could you say a secret word when you come this time? You can say pepper cake house – then I will know that you're the real Santa, because I don't want dad to be Santa. I also have a bird, its white and called Pippi-Marie. Can I ask you something! Why do you change clothes in our basement? Why do you wear a mask? Why do you wear a different suit when you're at our neighbor's place? Write soon,

I want a stamp from the North Pole.

Regards Janne, NORWAY.

In Russia, Santa Claus is known as "Father Frost".

Dear Santa Claus,

I don't know where we will be on Christmas Eve, we have grand parents and uncles and aunts, and mum and dad haven't decided yet. Therefore I'm going to write you my cell phone number so you can call me when you're on your way. Is that okay?

Regards Timothy, ENGLAND.

Dear Santa Claus,

Do you borrow a lot of the reindeer from the Sami? Are they wild or tamed reindeer? How much do you pay to rent them?

Regards Matthew, SCOTLAND.

Dear Santa Claus,

My name is Ikve and I am 12 year old Japanese student. I don't want a lot of things but I have question that I would like you to answer if you have time: How do you manage to navigate in the clouds? Do you do it yourself or do the reindeer do it? If they do it, how do they know where to go?

Yours Ekve, JAPAN.

Pour Noël, Madame, Monsieur,

Is it possible for me, in a few years time, to become a female president or a prime minister of this country?

Sincerely Charlotte, FRANCE.

Dear Santa,

What do you do when you land on a roof of an apartment block? Because you can't climb down all the chimneys, because you don't know who you get to?

Lots of greetings from Grete, GERMANY.

Dear Father Christmas,
I've been absolutely kind as an angel this year.
So I'll get bigger presents, won't I?
Yours Prescelli, ENGLAND.

Dear Santa,
My name is Terunori, and I live in Japan. I am
a member of a Judo club. Do you practice Judo,
or do you prefer karate?
Yours Terunori, JAPAN.

Dear Santa Claus,
What's it like in the North Pole? Do you have a reindeer
called Chake? How old are you? I only want one thing for
Christmas, and that is a doorbell for the door to my room
so I can have a little privacy. What's your favorite food?
Does it always snow up there? Are there two people out
there called Heatmizer or Snowmizer? I hope that you'll
have a wonderful, peaceful and relaxing Christmas! Can
you ensure me that my family is safe this Christmas?
Yes, and then I would like a puppy as a present. Have a
safe trip and a very Merry Christmas!
Your friend Megan, USA.

Dear Santa Claus,
I have something to ask you. Where do
you get all the presents from? And the money for all
the presents? Do you use the latest high tech
equipment, or do you use old gear?
Love Wayne, MALAYSIA.

Dear Santa,
Is it possible to become your Japanese friend?
Yours Tomomi, JAPAN.

Caro Babbo Natale,
Can I come and help you next Christmas? Will you
pay for my trip or can you come and get me?
Yours Isabel, ITALY.

Dear Santa Claus,
Is it possible to send you a list of what I want for the next
five Christmases? Then you can sort out presents
according to what you have in store. Please write me
back, I hope you say yes!
Best wishes William, ENGLAND.

Natale 2008

CarissiMO
Babbo NaTAle

sono la piccola Ilaria "Piky" e ti scrivo
questa letterina perché, anche se ho fatto
qualche volta la birbaoa, vorrei che tu
mi portassi i regali !
All' asilo mi comporto bene e dicono che
faccio la brava; a casa con il mio fratellino
Lorenzo, la mamma e il papà sono

Hello Santa,

Do you believe in God? Do you go to church?
Do you really come down the chimney?
Christmas greetings from Ida, NORWAY.
PS: I am not stupid!

Dear Santa,
Can you deliver animals as Christmas presents?
Do you have any animals in the North Pole, like parrots,
dogs, cats, guinea pig, horses, or mini pigs?
From Kathy, USA.

Dear Santa Claus,
I write to you for the first. My interests are riding
and sleeping. What are yours? Can I communicate
with you from my heart?
Sincerely Akiko, JAPAN.

Dear Santa,
Do you have blue lights on your sledge (or red)?
Do you also have sirens?
Regards Jim, NEW ZEALAND.

Dear Santa Claus,

My name is Myriam and I am eight years old. Is it true that you have nine reindeer? Is it true that their names are: Dasher, Dancer, Prancer, Vixen, Comet, Cupid, Donner, Blixen and Rudolph? My post box is 30, and I want two Barbie dolls and a Barbie man, ten fairytale books and two chocolates.

Sincerely Myriam, TANZANIA.

Dear Santa,

How are you? My name is Junna. I'm a third year student at Koromu elementary school. My birthday is March 19th, so please write me back – on my birthday! I have more questions. Will you answer them? Here they are: Where do you live? What's your full name? How long is your sledge? How old are you? What do you do (your job?). Please answer these questions and take care!

Junna, JAPAN.

Dear Mr. Santa Claus,

Merry Christmas! My name is Tomoya and I am eleven years old. Would you come to Japan? Do you like Japanese children?

Love Tomoya, JAPAN.

Dear Santa Claus,

You live on the North Pole? Do you like playing snowball? And do you like making snowmen? I think I will like to visit you on the North Pole when I grow up, okay? Good health and merry Christmas!

From your Wain, HONG KONG.

PS: My China name is Yeung.

Dear Santa Claus,

Is it okay if I call you? What's your phone number? What's you favourite color? How many presents do you have room for on your sledge? My name is Kelly, and I have long hair and blue eyes and a long face. I have white skin and two sisters. If you like, I would like to have many games, some shoes, a leather jacket and a violin box. I hope you can deliver all the presents, and that you deliver to England, and be careful you don't smash presents. I enjoyed writing to you.

Yours hopefully Kelly, ENGLAND.

140

Dear Santa Claus,

How are you? It's fun to write to you. My name is Mari, and I like you. But why didn't you come to me on Christmas Eve? Why not? Well, what do you do in the summer? That's my question. Please answer my request. I also want a picture of you. And I want to go to your house and meet you. Write me when you can.

Love Mari, JAPAN.

Dear Santa Claus,

Merry Christmas and happy New Year's. I'll appreciate knowing if you're ready for Christmas now? Have you seen all the presents? My name is Raphael and I'm nine years old. I like Christmas very much, and dad and I put all the presents under the tree. Ho! Ho! Ho! Santa. Can I please have a big football net and a Playstation. I appreciate writing to you, and please give the homeless children some toys.

Yours Raphael, ENGLAND.

Dear Mr. Santa,

How are you, Mr. Santa? My name is Shiho, and I'm from Kasai in Japan. First I would like to ask you a question. Why does Mr. Santa only come at winter time? Can I see you one day? I'm happy to receive presents every year.

Love Shiho, JAPAN.

Dear Santa Claus,

How are you? My name is Yuko. I'm 14 years old. I have never seen you so I would like to meet you. My house doesn't have a chimney. Can you come inside my house without a chimney? Please give me a present. I would like a big Christmas tree. Have a nice Christmas!

From Yuko, JAPAN.

Dear Santa Claus,

How many pixies live in Norway? Are you related to all of them? Or is it only you, your wife and kids? I want a lot of snow for Christmas, but that may be difficult since we never have snow here. But what about a portable computer?

Greetings from Bob, USA

Hello,

Nice to meet you. We're a group of Japanese high school students. Norway is a very cold country, right? We've never been there, but wish to go there at any price. We want to ask you some questions: Do you really come into people's houses through the chimney? Did your bum ever get stuck inside the chimney? What number Santa are you? Are you a Christian? We are Buddhist. How many reindeer do you have? We're looking forward to your answer. We can briefly introduce you to Japan. Japan is surrounded by water and the tallest mountain is called "Mt. Fuji". Japanese food is called "washoku". Do you understand a little Japanese? Please, come to Japan and give us presents!

Goodbye from Miko, JAPAN.

Dear Santa Claus,

I wonder if it's you who put candy in my sock? I'm 10 years old and believe you exist, but there are hardly any boys who believe in you, but if you write me back, I'll tell them that you exist. I want one thing most of all, and that's a Caso magic diary, I've wanted that for a long time. I'll write to you every year.

Love Susan, NORWAY.

Dear Santa Claus,

What are you doing right now? Do you receive a lot of letters these days? Is the sledge ready for Christmas? If not your reindeer probably won't ride it, do you think? Say hi to them from me. Could I please have some CDs and a dictionary for my computer?

Yours Kerry, ENGLAND.

Dear Santa,

My name is Sakie, and I'm 14 years old. I like cakes, what kind of food do you like the best? Do you make all the presents for the children yourself?

From Kajitani, JAPAN.

Dear Santa Claus,

Do you say 'Ho! Ho! Ho!' because you don't speak other languages that your own? Is that the reason you only say 'Ho! Ho! Ho!'?

Greetings from Paulina, POLAND.

Hallo lieber Weihnachtsmann!

Ich wünsche Dir ein schönes
Weihnachtsfest.
Ich habe einen großen
Wunsch. Kannst Du
mir ein kleines Gedicht
auf norwegisch schreiben?
Vielleicht kann ich
es ja lernen.
Dankeschön
und viele Grüße auch
an Deine Helfer!

Deine Anja aus Rostock

DEAR SANTA

Dear Santa,

Hallo, Santa. How are you? My name is Mayumi, I'm Japanese. I'm 15 years old. Can I ask you a few questions? Where do you live? What color do you like best? How tall are you? Do you like Japan? Thanks a lot. English and math are my worst subjects.

Goodbye from Mayumi, JAPAN.

Dear Santa Claus,

Do you wear a parachute when you fly Christmas Eve, or do you have a catapult like jet planes?

Love André, BELGIUM.

Dear Santa,

How old are the kids when you stop giving them presents? Are you the richest man in the world or is there a secret agreement between you and the parents?

Yours Horst, GERMANY.

Mr. Santa Claus,

Do you have any Panasonic products in store?

From Miku, JAPAN.

Dear Santa Claus,

My name is Rie and I'm 15 years old. I live in Japan. How old are you? Where do you live? I wish to know everything about you. Can your reindeer fly in the sky? I would like to ride them. Well, do the reindeer have your name? Please tell me about them. Last...

I would like a star!

From Rie, JAPAN.

Dear Santa Claus,

Is it OK if I call you Santa Claus? I hope so. Do you like Christmas? And are you ready for it? Are you fine? I'm fine, and I hope you're fine too. Do you like football? My favorite team is Manchester United, what's yours? Do you have advent calendars in Norway? How do you manage to travel around the world in one night? Because it'll take you more than 12 hours. And one more thing, I don't believe in Santa or Saint Nicholas. What day do you spent Christmas? And what night? Are you very busy? Do you have any children and do you enjoy Christmas? Is it incredibly hard to travel around in one night? For Christmas this year I don't want a lot of presents, and I wish you a fine day.

Yours hopefully Claire, ENGLAND.

Dear Santa Claus,
Are you and Bill Gates related, or do you work together? Have you been on vacation together? Are you richer than him?
Love Susan, USA.

Dear Santa Claus,
Do you get so angry with people that you don't give them any Christmas presents?
Regards, Marit, NORWAY.

Dear Santa Claus,
How are you? What's your email address?
Love Selamanit, ETHIOPIA.

Dear Santa,
I'm 14 years old. How old are you? My hobby is watching TV. What's your hobby? I like baseball, what about you? What food do you like the most? I like Sushi best.
From Masuda, JAPAN.

Dear Santa Claus,

Everybody says that I'm too old to believe in you, but there's got to be something good in this great unhappy world where billions live with war, hunger and poverty. Therefore I've decided than the good thing is you. Don't stress too much so you end up all burned out, and that's not so good. And then I'm wondering about one thing: Does Santa get presents too?

Hugs from Cathrine 16 years old, NORWAY.

Caro Babbo Natale,

Do you have many different names, or do you have sibling? Who's Santa Claus, and who's Father Christmas? Is Father Christmas the name of a month, and if so, which one?

Love Samuele, ITALY.

Dear Santa Claus,

Would you like to live in a hot, tropical zone, or do you prefer to live up in the North Pole?

Greetings from Mikael, RUSSIA.

Dear Santa Claus,

Nice meeting you. My name is Tsuyoshi and I want to ask you some questions. In which way do you deliver the presents around the world? Can wish for something from you? Would you like to bring me my Christmas present in person? I'll appreciate having your signature and a letter. Well, have a good time. Send me some words!

From Tsuyoshi, JAPAN.

Dear Santa Claus,

How old are you? I'm 15 years old, do you remember my house? Do you like The Beatles? I like John Lennon the most. Can you really fly? How often have you had parts in movies? I think Charlie Sheen is cute. What about you? Do you think Winona Ryder is nice and really pretty? I love her. Please visit my house and give me a present this year.

Goodbye. Regards from Kenta, JAPAN.

Dear Santa Claus,

I wonder about a lot of things, for example: How long do your reindeer live? Do you change them when they get old? How can you tell when they're worn out and no longer able to fly fast anymore? How do you ride them, is it like riding a horse? Dog sledges need a leader dog, do you have a leader reindeer? How do you know if they're hungry or thirsty when you fly over the roofs? Do you bring food and drinks in the sledge, or is it nice people who feed them? Looking forward to your answer! Greetings from Gillion, BELGIUM.

Dear Santa Claus,

I want to buy a spider in a pet shop, so tell me that you'll come there first and pay for it. The shop closes early on Christmas Eve. Is that alright? Regards Nathan, ENGLAND.

Dear Santa Claus,

Do you fly straight to Japan or do you land anywhere in between? From Masaki, JAPAN.

P.S: My dad is a pilot and lands several times.

Hello Santa,

You're nice and it's great when you visit. I believe in pixies. I would like a doll make up face. Aunt Jorun has several in her shop; could you Santa come to the shop and find suggestions for presents?

Regards, Marita, NORWAY.

Dear Santa Claus,

My name's Akane, and I'm 15 years old. My constellation is Cancer and my blood type is A. Many people say "Santa doesn't exist", but I believe in you. Therefore I'm writing to you; I like Santa's Christmas story very much because it gives the entire world good dreams. I like animals very much, and think your reindeer are noble. What other animals live with you? Can we pat them when we come and visit?

Greetings from Akane, JAPAN.

Dear Santa Claus,

Does your reindeer bite when you pet them, and do they wear a bridle when they're flying? By the way, what do you do when they fly and have to relieve themselves?

Greetings from Vilde, NORWAY.

Dear Santa,
Do you play the clarinet?
Best wishes Misa, JAPAN.

Dear Santa Claus,
My dad and granddad are bald. If that's heritable,
will I become bald? Are you bald?
From Jens, DENMARK.

Dear Santa,
Do you dare play hockey against me
if I come to Norway?
Love Aya, JAPAN.

Dear Santa Claus,
How do you protect yourself from crashing in the air?
Because there's a lot of planes up there?
Love Samuel, ENGLAND.

Santa Claus,
Why don't I get a hairdryer from you for Christmas?
I wanted one last year and the year before, but I
didn't receive one. Now both my sisters have their
own hairdryers, and how long will I have to
borrow theirs? Could you tell me?
Love Ewa, POLAND.

Dear Santa Claus,
Where are you going on summer vacation next year?
Love Nozomi, JAPAN.

Dear Santa Claus,
What command words do you tell your reindeer?
Is it difficult, or are they so clever that they
understand what you say to them?
Kind regards Albert, POLAND.

Dear Santa Claus,
I don't believe in you right now, but if you
really exist you could send me a postcard?
Yours Kimura, JAPAN.

Dear Father Christmas,
Hello, how are you? I'm an Italian girl from Concordia,
a small town near Modena. I'm happy, are you also
happy? My favorite number is 500, what's yours?
My favorite color is purple, what's yours?
My favorite animal is a cat, and yours?
Ciao, Veronica, ITALY.

Dear Santa Claus,
Does Rudolph and the other reindeer have blue noses when
they fly in the cold? Does it take a long or short time?
What color do they get after the reds?
Greetings Marie, FRANCE.

Dear Santa Claus,
I have a question for you. When you give us money, do
you print it yourself? And in that case isn't it false
money which is forbidden to spend?
Regards Sönke, GERMANY.

Dear Santa Claus,
Question for you: Have I been nice this year?
Greetings from Helene, NORWAY.

Dear Santa Claus,
Here in Japan you're pictured as Japanese. But your
address is in Norway where you live. Are you still
Japanese? Is your wife also Japanese?
Your friend Yuya, JAPAN.

Dear Santa Claus,
How long does a Christmas round take? How many
children get presents in one round?
Regards Kristóf, HUNGARY.

My dear Santa,
What do reindeer eat? Are they in their stables when you
don't use them, or do you lend them to the Samians?
Regards Jean, FRANCE.

Dear Santa Claus,

I write to you because I want to see you on Christmas day, and because I want to believe in you. I want to see you. I also want my friends to believe in you. In school today we talked about you, and when I told my friends that I believe in you, they started laughing and called me a sad person. That hurt me so, I was so sad that I went home and went to bed. Many kisses and hugs from Charlie, ENGLAND.

PS: Can I sit in your sledge, and can I say hello to all the reindeer?

Dear Santa Claus,
Have you ever been drunk?
Love Karin, GERMANY.

Dear Santa Claus,
I'm tired of my dad dressing up as Santa.
When are you going to come?
Christmas greetings from Mia Charlotte, NORWAY.

Dear Santa,

My name is Ligia, and I'm nearly 12 years old,
I live in Romania. I think about you every night now,
and Christmas Eve is my favorite evening because then
you come to our house and put presents under the tree. Do
you like milk and cookies? If so I'll place that on the
kitchen table. By the way – how are you? Hope you don't
have the flu. How's Rudolph, the red-nosed reindeer? And
how are the other reindeer? Speaking of presents... well,
I wish for a little snow and presents for my friends.
A thousand thanks!
Hugs from Ligia, ROMANIA.

Dear Santa Claus,
Do you like spaghetti?
Love Hikari, JAPAN.

Dear Santa Claus,
How long does it take for you to deliver all the
presents for the kids in Belgium?
Yours Gwen, BELGIUM.

DEAR SANTA

Dear Santa Claus,
My name is Alexander, can I open my presents before Christmas? Send some more presents, please. I'll put porridge out for you on Christmas Eve.
Yours Alexander, NORWAY.

Mr. Santa Claus,
Do you have some nice summer vacations? It is awfully hot in Japan. Take care, and I hope you appreciate my greeting. By the way, in the summer we like to eat water melon, ice cream and tomatoes in Japan. Goodbye!
From Sayuri, JAPAN.

Caro Babo Natale,
Are you a cosmonaut since you fly super fast around the world?
Greetings from Rosa, ITALY.

Cher Père Nöel,
When are you retiring? And who takes over after you?
From Lea, FRANCE.

Dear Santa,

Do you wear a parachute when you're flying? Do all the reindeer as well? Have you ever used them?

From Connor, SCOTLAND.

Dear Santa Claus,

Would you please send me a picture of you, Mrs. Santa and the reindeer? By email is fine, if you prefer that.

Yours Luke, CANADA.

Dear Santa Claus,

My name is Megumi, and I'm 18 years old. How are you? You must be really busy making presents? Good luck with all the work and I wish you good health and a good future in the years to come.

Love Megumi, JAPAN.

Dear Santa Claus,

Do you need an education to become Santa, or is it heritable?

Love Kenneth, NORWAY.

DEAR SANTA

Dear Sir,
Do you keep a file of all the children in the world – who's
been good or bad? If so, do you store it on a computer?
What program do you use?
From Luke, USA.

Dear Santa,
Merry Christmas. I like oranges, and I can swim.
Do you like oranges, and can you swim? My birthday
is June the 2nd, when's yours?
Regards Konomi, JAPAN.

Dear Santa Claus,
My name is María and I'm going to be 12 years old.
I sincerely want a dog. But I don't know which race.
I imagine a perfect dog, but it probably doesn't exist.
But I hope it's nice and obedient, but not too big.
Could you please tell me what race the perfect
dog is? Can you help me?
Love María, NORWAY.

Dear Santa Claus,
Do you belong to your own race or are you a
human being? If you're not a human being, can
you write to me and tell me about your race?
Many greetings from Phillip, GERMANY.

Hello Santa,
Do you think Mrs. Santa can come to our house
instead of you? I'm so scared of you, you see.
Sorry. Don't be sad, Santa.
Kiss from Jonas, NORWAY.

Dear Santa Claus,
Why do you constantly say "are there any nice children
here" when you know that I'm the only kid in the house?
From Lene, SWEDEN.

Dear Father Christmas,
Why can't I have a dog for Christmas just because
I already have a cat? I'm angry with you!
From Leon, HUNGARY.

Dear Santa Claus,
Do you have baby pigs in store? If I can wish for
a real baby pig from you, I do that, but you have
to handle it with mum and dad. OK?
Love Cicilia, SWEDEN.

Dear Santa Claus,
Do you hibernate in the winter, or do
you snore like a man?
From Steve, GREECE.

Dear Santa,
Can I have your phone number?
Love Ninomiya, JAPAN.

Dear Santa Claus,
What do you do if you get sick when you have to deliver
the presents? Does the Mrs bring them out instead? How
is she at riding a sledge, by the way?
Love Jason, USA.

Dear Santa...

Sad wishes

Dear Santa,

I write this to ask you if you can do something for me. I'm a single parent with two boys aged 10 and 11, and we live with my parents. Unfortunately I'm not capable of giving them any of the things they want for Christmas – and I've never known where to write for help before. Therefore I sincerely, utterly, strongly hope that you can give them some of the things they want in the letter they write to you. I would be so happy, so glad, if any of their wishes can come true. The boys have been disappointed and frustrated for many years, and they are really nice boys, believe me. I assume that you don't get a lot of letters from parents like me, and hope that you don't think that I'm stupid for writing this to you. I thank you very much, and wish you a good and merry Christmas.

Big hug from from Amanela, ENGLAND.

Dear Santa,

My name is Kumiko, and I'm from Japan. I'm 18 years old, but I don't have a girlfriend. I'm very lonely. That's why I write to you. I'll probably be alone this year too. I hope to have a wonderful Christmas.

From Kumiko, JAPAN.

Dear Santa Claus,
I wish to have my dad back who died last summer.
Yours Akis, GREECE.

Dear Father Christmas,
Soon Christmas arrives and I want my grandmother to regain her health. I know that you don't have enough power to help her, but my dear, could you land here when you fly by so she and I can see your wonderful reindeer and helpers? Thanks in advance!
Many greetings from Milka, SLOVAKIA.

Dear Santa Claus,
I'm not allowed to be home on Christmas Eve.
Could you please send some gifts on Friday 29th instead because then I'm home with my mother again and we'll celebrate Christmas?
Love Elida, NORWAY.

Dear Santa Claus,
I'm so lonely. I wish I had a piano I could play.
It's only me here in my apartment.
Kaori, HONG KONG.

Dear Santa Claus,
I wish dad would be nicer.
Greetings from Kjersti, NORWAY.

Dear Santa Claus,
I'm a Portuguese boy called Ricardo. I really want a bike
for Christmas. We don't have a papa, therefore we would
like to have a present from you.
Yours Ricardo, PORTUGAL.

In Spain children leave their shoes under the Christmas tree the
night of January 5th, and presents from the Three Kings (Los
Reyes Magos, Melcher, Gaspar and Baltasar) appear the next
morning. Santa Claus is called Papa Noel, and some children
receive presents both days on December 24th (from Papa Noel)
and on January 6th (from the Three Kings).